Rest Rise Reclaim

Leadership Lessons For
Black Women Who Lead

Beverley A. Powell

REST RISE RECLAIM

Authored by Beverley A. Powell

©Beverley A. Powell 2025

Edited by Marcia M Publishing House Editorial Team

Cover design, printing & binding: Marcia M Publishing House Ltd.

Published by Marcia M Spence of Marcia M Publishing House Ltd.

On behalf of Beverley A. Powell, In West Bromwich, West Midlands the UNITED KINGDOM B71.

All rights reserved 2025 Beverley A. Powell

Beverley A. Powell asserts the moral right to be identified as the author of this work. The opinions expressed in this published work are those of the author and do not reflect the opinions of Marcia M Publishing House or its editorial team.

This book is sold subject to the conditions it is not, by way of trade or otherwise, lent, hired out or otherwise circulated in any form of binding or cover other than that in which it is published. No part of this publication may be reproduced, stored in a retrieval system or transmitted in any form or by any means (electronic, mechanical, photocopying, recording or otherwise) without prior written permission from the Author.

ISBN: 978-1-9193441-0-2

A copy of this publication is legally deposited in The British Library.

www.marciampublishing.com

Dedication

To my foremothers —

For the women who came before me — my ancestors, my grandmothers, aunties, mothers, sisters, and daughters — who carried the weight of the world without recognition, whose voices were stifled, and whose brilliance was dimmed.

I write this as a Black woman standing at the threshold of a new chapter, reflecting on a lifetime of leadership, resilience, and hard-won wisdom.

This book is my offering to you — to those who fought, endured, and survived so that I could stand here, no longer bound by the need to be everything to everyone.

I speak because you could not. I rest because you were denied rest. I lead because you paved the way and, therefore, I stand on the shoulders of giants.

The women whose names I may never know, but whose strength lives within me.

You were silenced, stripped of your freedom, denied the right to grieve or rage.
Your beauty was hidden, your bodies used — commodified, exploited, and experimented on.
And yet, you endured.
You persisted with a resilience that transcends time.

Though the world denied your voice, I write this book in honour of your unbreakable spirit.
I stand on the foundation you laid, using the voice you were never allowed to raise.
This is my offering — a testament to your legacy, a reclaiming of what was always ours.

Ubuntu *— I am because we are.*

And to every Black woman today, especially those walking the often-silent path through menopause —
I see you.
I hear you.
I feel you.

May these pages affirm your worth, reflect your truth, and remind you:
You are not invisible. You are not alone.
You are powerful, precious, and whole — exactly as you are.

This book is for you.

Opening Remarks

This book offers a window into the unique experiences of the Black woman leading and navigating in different settings. Here I bear witness to my own unique experiences by sharing my vulnerabilities with you, the reader. Through my own reflections I open the window and share with you my own deep, sometimes painful journey of navigating systems of patriarchy and oppression that often leave us feeling like imposters in spaces we rightfully belong. By sharing these moments of doubt, struggle, and ultimate triumph, I aim to create a space where you, too, can see your own experiences mirrored and validated.

This book is not just my story; it is a testament to the collective challenges that we face as Black women. By offering my vulnerability, I hope to encourage you to embrace your own — recognising that in these honest, raw moments, we find the strength to heal, to rise, and continue forging paths in spaces that were never built for us but are forever changed by our experience. I explore the challenges we face, from navigating systemic barriers to balancing the weight of representation, while still finding joy and purpose. For those of you in leadership, this book offers a space to reflect on the emotional and mental toll that can often come with being a trailblazer, while also celebrating the strength, resilience, and wisdom that we carry. Through sharing my personal leadership journey, I hope to provide insights that will inspire and empower other Black women leaders to continue pushing boundaries, standing tall in their truth and power, and leading with grace and courage.

This book is not only a guide for healing but an offering of insights into navigating leadership within complex, bureaucratic systems that are invariably shaped around the white majority within systems. It is also a testament to the triumphs and complexities of Black women, part of the global majority in leadership, offering support and solidarity in spaces where we are often underrepresented yet undeniably impactful.

This book is grounded in historical context and lived experience. It explores the challenges that continue to shape the lives of women in the UK — particularly Black women — with a specific lens on the north-west of England, where I spent my formative years. The legacy of colonisation, migration, slavery, and systemic racism is not distant history — it is deeply personal, woven through both my life and the lives of countless women of colour. These forces, along with key historical events during my lifetime, have shaped my worldview and leadership journey.

But this book is not solely about struggle. It honours the full spectrum of Black womanhood — our joy, love, creativity, and accomplishments. We are not a monolith. We are layered and multi-dimensional, shaped by culture, identity, and resilience. Within these pages, I also confront colourism within our communities and the ongoing tension between societal beauty standards and our own self-image — issues that have long shaped how we are seen and how we see ourselves.

Throughout this book, the importance of community runs like a golden thread. Employee staff network groups (ESNGs), sister circles, and informal networks have offered spaces of belonging, strength, and healing. I reflect on how these communities sustained me through shifting political, social, and economic landscapes, both in the UK and globally.

Introduction

Navigating the corporate world as a Black woman is a layered experience — shaped by race, gender, culture, and the unspoken rules of spaces never designed with us in mind. It is a journey marked by brilliance and burden, resilience and resistance. Yet, too often, our narratives are overlooked, simplified, or lost in research that fails to capture the richness and reality of our lived experiences.

As I sat with Black women in one-to-one coaching conversations and group development sessions, a familiar thread emerged — the persistent, quiet presence of **imposter syndrome**. Despite excellence, we questioned our worth. Despite achievements, we doubted our belonging. This wasn't individual insecurity — it was the emotional toll of navigating systems that constantly asked us to shrink, to prove, to endure.

This book was born from that truth.

It is both a call and a companion — an evidence-informed, heart-led offering to amplify our voices, honour our stories, and name not just the challenges, but the power, strategy, and joy we carry. This is about reclaiming our space, our leadership, and our right to rest.

Whether you are just beginning your journey, standing at a crossroads, or quietly folding up your Superwoman cape — may these pages remind you: you are not alone. You are not an imposter. You are more than worthy. Do not dim your light — shine your light bright.

Disclaimer

This book reflects my personal journey and lived experiences. It is not intended to represent the experiences of all individuals or groups, nor to make definitive claims about any person, community, or institution. While I have made every effort to share my story authentically and respectfully, any resemblance to individuals, events, or circumstances is purely coincidental and unintentional unless explicitly stated.

I acknowledge that everyone's experiences are unique, and my reflections are deeply rooted in my perspective. If any part of this work is perceived as referencing a specific person or group in a way that was not intended, I offer my sincerest apologies. This book is written with the aim of fostering understanding, growth, and shared humanity.

Leadership Lessons For Black Women Who Lead

Beverley A. Powell

Preface

Writing this book has been more than simply putting pen to paper — it has been a soulful act of liberation, a deliberate and courageous turning of lived experience into leadership wisdom. It marks the culmination of years spent unlearning, reframing, truth-telling, and reclaiming power on my own terms — not the ones imposed upon me by systems, expectations, or history.

For years, people would say, "You really should write a book." I heard them — but life had other plans. The path to this point has not been easy. I've navigated profound personal losses, career shifts, returning to study, relocating across the UK alone, a global health crisis, and the emotional physical and mental upheaval of the menopause — a roller coaster that stole sleep, hijacked energy, and tested my spirit, I'm still here, with more clarity, more softness, and now — finally — the permission to write.

At first, I imagined this book would flow easily. I thought I could keep it professional, stay in my head, and stick to theory. But my personal book coach, a true champion, gently challenged me to go deeper. She urged me to move from head to heart — to be vulnerable, real, and bold. That was no easy feat. Some leadership experiences were buried too deep and were too painful to revisit. But as I stand at the threshold of retirement, reflecting on a career built over decades, I feel ready. Ready to tell the truth to myself and read it on paper. Ready to pass on what I've learned. Ready to burn the Superwoman cape.

Yes – the metaphor is intentional. For too long, I wore that invisible cape, showing strength while carrying the weight of expectation. I was "resilient", "strong", and "unshakable" – because the world demanded it of me as a Black woman, and because I had learned to demand it of myself.

But strength without rest is exploitation. Resilience without vulnerability is a mask. And the time has come to let go of this performance and embrace a different kind of power – one rooted in softness, in imperfection, in being fully human.

In writing this book, I also recognised the need to bring clarity to the language that underpins many of the conversations within it. Words like *intersectionality*, *reparation*, and *systemic racism* are not just academic terms – they are lived realities for Black women, particularly when navigating the silent and shame-filled terrain of imposter syndrome. Towards the end of this book, I've included a dedicated glossary to offer context and understanding – so all readers, regardless of background, can journey through these pages with shared insight.

This book is for the Black woman in the thick of the menopause – disoriented, dismissed, and perhaps even doubting herself. It's for the young Black girl on the cusp of career and ambition, unsure of her voice in rooms not designed for her. It's for the well-meaning white manager who wants to support their Black staff with empathy, not pity. And it's for the healthcare professional sitting across from an anxious

Black woman patient, seeking not only to heal, but to *understand*. Black women feel pain. Black women cry. Black women laugh and know joy — but only in spaces where it feels safe to do so.

This book has been a deeply personal and transformative process — a catharsis, a celebration, a letting go. These pages carry memories, leadership lessons, painful truths, and precious moments of grace. I don't pretend to speak for every Black woman — our stories are richly diverse. As Chimamanda Ngozi Adichie reminds us in her TED Talk — 'The Danger of a Single Story' — no one voice is enough. But in sharing mine, I hope you'll find something that resonates.

This is my journey. And it's time to rise, rest, and reclaim.

Beverley A. Powell

As I stand fully in my truth, free from the weight of the Superwoman cape, I am clear about who I am and how I choose to lead. This manifesto is my declaration — a commitment to myself and to those who walk a similar path.

There comes a time in every woman's journey when she must define herself on her own terms. After years of wearing the Superwoman cape, I decided to lead, to rest, to thrive without apology. This manifesto is my declaration of who I am and how I choose to move through the world. It is my promise to myself and an invitation to you: to stand firm in your truth, to release the burdens never meant to be yours, and to embrace the life and leadership you deserve.

My Personal Manifesto

I am a Black British woman, a leader, a coach, and a guide for those navigating spaces not built with them in mind. My journey has been shaped by resilience, wisdom, and the unwavering belief that I am enough — without the weight of the Superwoman cape.

I Choose

- To lead with authenticity, knowing my presence and voice matter.
- To reject imposter syndrome and step boldly into every space, not seeking permission but owning my right to be there.

I Commit

- To uplifting and empowering women — especially Black women — so they see their brilliance reflected to them.

- To challenge systems, policies, and mindsets that diminish our worth and to rewrite the narratives imposed upon us.

I Believe

- That joy, rest, and boundaries are acts of self-preservation, not indulgence.

- That my well-being is non-negotiable – exhaustion is not a badge of honour, and sacrifice is not a measure of success.

I Honour

- My lived experiences – the struggles, the triumphs, and the moments of doubt – transforming them into lessons that inspire and ignite change.

- My menopause journey, using my voice to dismantle stigma and advocate for workplaces that respect and support women at every stage of life.

I Declare

- That my legacy will not be one of silent endurance, but of fearless leadership, radical self-acceptance, and unwavering commitment to those who come after me.

This is who I am. This is how I lead. This is how I rise.

This is my guiding light, but what is yours? I encourage you to write your own manifesto – one that honours your values, your journey, and your vision for the future. You do not need permission to take up space, to rest, to lead boldly. The world is waiting for you to show up as your fullest self. Are you ready?

Ubuntu: I am Because We Are

Can you be your own liberation?

Growing up as the eldest child in a single-parent household often felt like a lifelong apprenticeship in leadership. I became the second parent, the 'Lieutenant' to the 'General' — my mother. Our household was a battleground of domestic duties, where I led the charge in deputising for the cooking, preparing, and shopping for necessary household goods. Like many 'latchkey kids' of the 60s, I recognised the unspoken rule: the eldest child endured the most responsibility. Yet, this meant my needs as a child were not always met. To survive, I abandoned myself — my needs, my joy, my laughter. I ruled by head only, with my heart carefully tucked away as a protective mechanism. This abandonment of my own feelings became the groundwork for my journey into adulthood and senior leadership.

My Core Values

These values sit at the heart of this book — and at the heart of me. They are not abstract words, but lived truths shaped by my journey as a Black woman navigating leadership, identity, and healing.

Each value represents a conscious choice: to lead with authenticity, to rest without guilt, to embrace vulnerability, and to honour legacy. They reflect what I've had to reclaim after shedding the Superwoman cape, and what continues to guide me as I walk forward.

You'll see these values echoed throughout the stories, lessons, and leadership insights that follow. I share them with the hope that they will resonate with your own journey — and perhaps inspire you to reflect on the values that hold you up, too.

- **A — Authentic Empowerment**

Stay true to yourself while empowering others to lead boldly and unapologetically.

- **R — Resilient Joy**

Embrace rest and joy as acts of resistance and resilience, sustaining your leadership and well-being.

- **I — Inclusive Vulnerability**

Lead with courage and vulnerability, fostering trust and connection through compassion for yourself and others.

- **S — Self-Compassion**

Extend kindness and understanding to yourself, rejecting perfectionism, and embracing your worth.

- **E — Equality and Legacy**

Celebrate Black liberation and commit to building a legacy of inclusion, joy, and equality for future generations.

Overview

In authoring this book, I have taken a theory-of-change approach which has enabled me to plan and shape the contents.

What is my "WHY" for authoring this book? Over the years I have read, been inspired and motivated by several international Black women leaders, creatives, and authors. I authored this book with the younger me in mind and for the young Black girl from the north-west of England who embarked on making life-changing career choices. The contents of this book may also be insightful and speak to the wider Black women sisterhood and the non-Black manager or coach, male or female, who has never managed a diverse team or whose circle of close-knit friends outside the workplace look like themselves, albeit from the same race and socio-economic background.

Unmasking Self-Doubt: The Origins of the Imposter Syndrome

"Being a Black woman writer is not a shallow place, but a rich place to write from. It does not limit my imagination; it expands it. It is richer than being a white male writer because I know more, and I have experienced more." Toni Morrison

The imposter syndrome was first identified in 1978 by psychologist Dr Pauline Clance and Dr Suzanne Imes. It refers to the persistent feeling of inadequacy or self-doubt despite evidence of success or accomplishments. Originally, their research focused on high-achieving women who, despite their qualifications and achievements, felt they had "fooled" others into overestimating their abilities. Clance and Imes noticed that these women often attributed their success to luck or external factors rather than their own competence. This phenomenon has since been observed across various demographics, but its origins lie in the examinations of the internalised pressures and societal expectations placed on women, which contribute to this overwhelming sense of being an imposter in professional or academic spaces.

My key criticism of the original imposter syndrome study by Clance and Imes is its lack of diversity, particularly regarding race and socio-economic background. This research focused on white, middle and upper-class women, excluding the perspectives of Black women and other marginalised groups of women. This oversight limits the applicability of the research findings and the experiences of Black women, who face unique challenges stemming from the intersection of race and gender. Black women often contend with systemic racism, microaggression, and cultural expectations in addition to gender-based pressures, all of which can exacerbate feelings of inadequacy in ways that differ from the experiences of white women.

Furthermore, the study did not fully consider the socio-economic diversity of participants, omitting working-class women who may experience imposter syndrome differently due to economic inability and class barriers. For Black women, these intersecting identities mean that imposter syndrome is not just about individual self-doubt but is deeply tied to external societal structures that undermine our sense of belonging, worth, value and respect. Therefore, I am writing about imposter syndrome to shed light on the often overlooked and underexplored experiences of Black women, particularly in professional environments.

My own journey through this topic deepened when I was invited to design and deliver a workshop on imposter syndrome at an NHS conference in 2023 aimed at Black women employed within the health and social care system. Through this intervention, I gathered valuable insights from participants revealing that Black women's experiences of imposter syndrome are profoundly shaped by the intersection of race, gender compounded by the systemic barriers they face in white institutions such as the NHS. The outcomes from my research following the event emphasised the necessity of addressing these unique challenges. Many participants reported the feelings of being an imposter were not solely internal but reinforced by external factors such as microaggressions, racial bias and a lack of representation in senior leadership roles. This led to a deeper understanding that imposter syndrome, for Black women, cannot be adequately addressed without acknowledging the broader context of institutionalised racism and gender discrimination.

My decision to unashamedly aim this book at Black women stems from the belief that our voices, stories, and challenges need dedicated space for exploration. Too often, discussions around imposter syndrome have been generalised, failing to capture the complexity of Black women's experiences. By focusing my book on Black women and my own experiences, I hope to provide tools for empowerment, validation, and community support, while I also challenge the structures which contribute to these feelings of inadequacy. My book is both a response to the gaps in existing literature and an affirmation of the unique experiences Black women face in navigating spaces that often question their sense of belonging.

Is Imposter Syndrome Applicable to Black Women, or Is This More About Oppression?

Is imposter syndrome the right framework for understanding the challenges of Black women in leadership, or does it risk obscuring the systemic oppression at the heart of these challenges? Moreover, who am I to argue that a Black woman attending such a workshop is 'wrong' in seeking support through this lens?

Imposter Syndrome: A Brief Overview

Imposter syndrome describes an internalised belief that success is attributable to luck or external factors rather than ability, often accompanied by a fear of being exposed as inadequate. Initially studied in high-achieving women in the 1970s, the concept has since broadened to encompass individuals across various demographics.

However, critiques of imposter syndrome argue that it often fails to address how systemic inequities — like racism, sexism, and classism — play a significant role in fostering such feelings for marginalised groups, including Black women.

The Intersection of Oppression and Imposter Syndrome

For Black women, the experience of imposter syndrome is deeply intertwined with systemic oppression. Familiar challenges include:

- **Tokenism**: Operating as "the only" or "one of the few" in white or male spaces can amplify feelings of scrutiny and inadequacy.

- **Bias and Microaggressions**: Persistent exposure to stereotypes and implicit biases erodes confidence, making even the most capable individuals question their worth.

- **Lack of Representation**: The absence of visible role models in leadership positions often fosters a sense of not belonging, which is mislabelled as imposter syndrome rather than systemic exclusion.

These challenges suggest that what is often framed as imposter syndrome may, in fact, be a rational response to navigating hostile or exclusionary environments.

Are Black Women Wrong to Engage with Imposter Syndrome?

It is neither helpful nor ethical to dismiss the experiences of Black women who identify with imposter syndrome as a framework for understanding their struggles. If a Black woman chooses to attend a workshop on this topic, her decision should be met with respect, not criticism. Here's why:

1. **Personal Agency**: Individuals use the frameworks available to make sense of their lived experiences. If a Black woman finds the concept of imposter syndrome helpful, it is not for others to argue that she is wrong.

2. **Validation and Community**: Workshops on imposter syndrome often provide spaces for shared experiences and mutual support. For Black women, these spaces can be vital for fostering solidarity and resilience, even if the root causes of their struggles lie in oppression.

3. **A Gateway to Deeper Exploration**: While the term 'imposter syndrome' may not fully capture the intersection of race, gender, and systemic inequality, it offers a starting point for

conversation. Skilled facilitators can bridge this gap by contextualising the imposter syndrome within the broader realities of structural inequality.

A Nuanced Argument

The central question is not whether Black women should or should not experience imposter syndrome but whether the term adequately encapsulates their lived realities. The challenge is that imposter syndrome tends to frame self-doubt as an individual failing, rather than a response to systemic inequities such as racism and sexism.

To bridge the gap between the definition of imposter syndrome and the effective delivery of workshops and discussions tailored to Black women, I have outlined the following recommendations. These points are intended to guide anyone designing and delivering such workshops:

> **Recommendations**
>
> **Acknowledge Oppression**: Recognise systemic factors — like racism, sexism, and tokenism — that underpin feelings of inadequacy.
>
> **Empower Through Context**: Provide tools for resilience while affirming the validity of Black women's experiences in oppressive systems.
>
> **Encourage Collective Healing**: Move beyond individual responsibility to focus on structural change and shared empowerment.

Summary

While imposter syndrome in isolation risks pathologising Black women's responses to systemic oppression, it can still serve as a valuable entry point for exploring self-doubt. The key lies in expanding the conversation to connect subjective experiences with systemic realities. Rather than dismissing Black women who engage with the concept, we must honour their agency while creating space for personal growth and systemic critique.

My personal story as a working-class northern Black woman is central to this book because it offers an authentic and unique lived experience of navigating imposter syndrome within the unique context of race, gender, class, and region. In sharing my journey, I aim to connect with Black women who may feel isolated in their struggles, showing that they are not alone in the challenges they may face.

My own experiences of self-doubt, fighting to be seen, heard and validated led to a questioning of my self-worth in professional spaces, and confronting societal biases affect the broader themes of this book, a personal lens through which to explore imposter syndrome and the need to wear my Superwoman cape in a way that may be deeply relatable to other Black women. Sharing my personal story brings credibility and an emotional depth to the discussion and my arguments. It allows me to illustrate how deeply rooted these feelings can be, not just as a theoretical concept but as a real, lived phenomenon that affects every aspect of one's personal and professional identity. By weaving my experiences through the book, I highlight the intersections of race, gender and class, offering readers a mirror to reflect on their own lives while also providing strategies that have enabled me to move past these challenges and into transformation.

My story serves as testament to the power of resilience, reflection, and reclaiming one's narrative. By owning and sharing my experiences, I hope to inspire Black women to confront and dismantle the internalised doubts which may hold them back, and to see themselves as deserving of every opportunity and achievement they have earned.

My story provides a unique perspective of a second-generation Jamaican/Black British child raised in a working-class part of Greater Manchester, navigating the complexities of identity, culture, social class, and opportunity within the north-west of England. My story is set against a backdrop of pre government 1976 race relations Act explicit racism, multiculturalism and the northern working-class experience during the 1960's. This book offers a compelling narrative which explores the nuances of being a Black British working lass from outside of London. What sets my story apart is its exploration of the distinctive challenges and triumphs faced by a Black woman from the north of England, contrasting with narratives often centred around the south of England.

However, despite the geographical differences, my book uncovered striking commonalities shared by Black women across the UK in leadership roles, as they navigate through large bureaucratic systems. This book highlights the resilience, creativity, and determination of Black women in carving out their paths within institutional frameworks, fostering a deeper understanding of their experiences and contributions to society.

After over forty years of employment across various corporate public sector systems and leadership and management in the commercial world, having transitioned through the menopause, I find myself looking down the barrel of retirement at the end of a fulfilling and rewarding career in service of others. The time is now right to author a book about how I have burnt my Superwoman cape and found liberation, enabling me to embrace a true and authentic life.

Through many years of research and personal reflection—and especially during the last twenty years as a life coach supporting others, and more recently as a licensed menopause champion working with women of colour—I have come to understand the significant harm caused by suppressing emotions. When feelings are not fully processed, they tend to accumulate internally, impacting the body, particularly in high-stress environments. As Dr. Gabor Maté explains in When the Body Says No: Exploring the Stress—Disease Connection. Vintage Canada, (2003). The body retains the memory of what the mind attempts to repress.

Coaching from the Lens of Whiteness

Coaching from the Lens of Whiteness

While writing this book, I have kept in mind the white coach and the white manager who may be leading a diverse team for the first time and seeking to understand how to create a psychologically safe environment. This book offers insights and a practical roadmap to support cultural development and inclusive leadership.

I have chosen to focus on the unique experiences of Black women in the UK, particularly through the lens of imposter syndrome. Although imposter syndrome is often described as a common experience among women in general, I argue that the challenges faced by Black women differ profoundly from those encountered by their white counterparts. These differences arise from the intersection of race, gender, and societal expectations, which intensify feelings of inadequacy and, frequently, exclusion.

For the purposes of this book, being Black in the UK means navigating spaces where one's identity is often questioned or marginalised. This reality generates specific forms of self-doubt and external pressure that must be acknowledged in any meaningful conversation about imposter syndrome. Through this perspective, I aim to demonstrate why we cannot assume that all women experience imposter syndrome in the same way.

This book intricately delves into the unique experiences of my own first-hand experiences as a Black girl and Black woman coming to the end of her corporate working career.

As a Black woman, there are many shared cultural experiences. These historical trajectories have helped to profoundly shape my identity, and how I have dealt with the many challenges and celebrated the many triumphs.

While I lay down the foundations to this book, it is important to note how the economic landscape and industrial history of the north-west of England has enabled me to provide some context and compelling backdrop. Against the British legacy of industrialisation, coupled with post-industrial transformations, I have also been influenced by the social—economic opportunities, racial dynamics, and community resilience in distinct ways which have shaped my aspirations, and my societal role. By focusing on the north-west of England, this book illuminates the complex interplay and the impact on my life today as a Black woman of Jamaican heritage raised in Lancashire/Greater Manchester.

Moreover, while this book is aimed at sharing my lived experience as a Black woman, the north of England's cultural milieu — characterised by its own traditions, dialects, music, food and artistic expressions — also fosters a unique form of my identity, which has played a part in my life up to today and will never leave me.

Through storytelling and language which is culturally specific to the north-west, this book offers a textured understanding of how place shapes my complex identity and lived experience as a Black woman who has lived in that region.

By centring on the north-west, this book delves into the nuances of a Black woman's reality within a regional context, highlighting intersections of race, gender, social class, health, and place-based identities in ways which resonate authentically within the diverse landscapes and narratives of the region where I was raised.

Inclusive Spaces: Music Place and Social Change

The book also delves into the profound impact of Black music on the north-west's regional music scene, creating vibrant cultural hubs which drew in others from across the wider country, seeking unique musical experiences.

As a teenager in the 70s, the fusion of Black musical genres such as jazz funk, Northern soul, Tamla Motown with fashion hairstyles such as Afros, flares, platform shoes, long leather coats, brogue shoes, as just some examples, gave rise to a distinctive northern subculture characterised by its energetic dancing. There was also vinyl collecting from the Manchester jazz funk record shop known as Spin In, and an underground club scene which I frequented. One such iconic example was Northern Soul Night at the Wigan Casino in the 1970s and 1980s, which became a mecca for Tamla Motown enthusiasts, Black and white, from across the UK. Sadly, the club closed its doors for the last time on 6 December, 1981. Another music club was Cassinelli's, the home of jazz funk in Standish, Wigan. Wigan Pier back in the 70s and 80s was another jazz funk venue.

These northern venues and Black northern jazz funk bands not only highlighted Black music, but also served as inclusive spaces where cultural exchange, artistic experimentation, and collective celebration thrived. My book delves into how these scenes reflected and shaped broader social dynamics, challenging stereotypes, fostering cross-cultural dialogue, and contributing to the north's reputation as a cultural melting pot and beacon of creative expression.

By spotlighting these distinctive northern music scenes and their impact on cultural identities and movements, the book highlights the interconnectedness of music, place and social change while underscoring the north's enduring influence on the UK's cultural landscape, distinct from the south of England's musical narratives and venues.

Leadership Lessons For
Black Women Who Lead

Beverley A. Powell

Table of Contents

Dedication iii
Opening Remarks v
Introduction viii
Preface xii
Overview xix
Chapter 1: The Early Years 1
Chapter 2 Under The Superwoman Cape. 32
Chapter 3: Workplace Navigating Solitude 54
Chapter 4: Double the Struggle: 97
Chapter 5 Reinvention: Burning My Superwoman Cape, ... 110
Chapter 6 Joy Creativity and Accomplishments 125
Chapter 7: Golden Rest a Black Woman's Journey to Renewal, Reparation, and Rediscovery 129
Chapter 8 The L.I.F.T. Model – Leadership Life Lessons for Thriving Beyond the Cape 148
Chapter 9: Case Studies 151
Chapter 10: Tips and Tools 154
Chapter 11: Final Thoughts After the Cape Is Burnt: Leadership Life Lessons .. 163
Chapter 12 *"Self-care is not self-indulgence, it is self-preservation."* 171
Chapter 13: Cultural Perspectives on Menopausal Women 175
Conclusion: Towards Holistic Reparation 188
About the Author 204
Additional Resources 206
Dear Reader, ... 207
Bibliography 209

Chapter 1
THE EARLY YEARS

BEVERLEY A. POWELL

Clarendon Parish in Jamaica holds a special place in my family's history. It is where my grandmother and grandfather were born, where they raised my mother and her sisters, and where their roots run deep before answering the 'call of the Mother Country' to rebuild Britain after World War II.

Nestled in central Jamaica, Clarendon was a vibrant yet rural parish during their time there between 1930 and 1958. Agriculture was at the heart of life, with sugar plantations dominating the economy. In the more rural villages, families like mine would have relied on small-scale farming, while May Pen, the parish capital, thrived as a hub of trade and commerce. This blend of pastoral and emerging urban life gave Clarendon its unique character – progressive yet deeply connected to the land and its traditions.

The climate was tropical, with warm weather year-round and distinct wet and dry seasons that shaped daily life. The fertile plains and lush riverbanks, including the Rio Minho, supported crops and livestock, contributing to the community's self-sufficiency.

Clarendon stood apart from other rural parishes with its growing infrastructure and the resilience of its people. Known for their industriousness and powerful sense of community, the residents were deeply rooted in shared cultural values and traditions. Life there was not just about survival; it was about connection, celebration, and pride in their identity. This heritage shaped my family's values, instilling in them a sense of perseverance and unity.

When my family eventually left the familiar warmth of Clarendon for the uncertainty of post-war Britain, they carried with them the lessons, traditions, and strength of their homeland. Clarendon's rhythms and culture continue to echo in my life, even as I write this, bridging our past to our present.

From my earlier years I recall always enjoying being among nature. I was fortunate to live in an area which had a vast expanse of greenery. The place where I lived seemed to pause, and nature took over. It was a favourite spot for many families on sunny days, when it buzzed with life. The park was called Leverhulme Park, the largest in the town of Bolton at this time, and a place where the annual school sports day was held. I would represent my school at athletics and compete against all the Bolton schools at the annual school event. I would often happily play in the park.

Lancashire was at this time dominated by the industrial landscape of 19th-century England and the dark legacy of slavery, producing vast quantities of cotton textiles that were renowned worldwide. However, as I know it now, the town was evidence of the legacy of the brutal institution of slavery. The raw cotton was sourced from the deep American South, which ensured a steady stream of cotton supplying the insatiable Lancashire cotton machines, so the wealth and progress of the county was built on ancestral bloodlines. It is a part of the Lancashire story which is often overlooked in the history of industrialisation. My town still was a busy centre of industry with its towering chimneys, and I remember the busy Bolton Market known as one of the best markets in the area.

Sunday was a typical Sunday, with my mother busy cooking breakfast. The aroma from the cooked sausages and the smell of grilled toast, margarine and eggs made my tummy rumble. I loved my mother's cooking. She was an exceptionally good cook. The smell of breakfast lingered in the air as I got myself ready for my Sunday trip out with my father. My thick, "good hair" (a term used in Jamaican circles when discussing Black women and children's hair) had been beautifully styled by my mother and parted into two neat, long, thick plaits finished off with two of my favourite hair ties, two red ribbons, which had gold-like threads running along the edge of each. I loved my ribbons. My mother bought many pairs of brightly coloured ribbons for me for that reason on Sundays, for Sunday school or special days out. On this day, I wore crisp white lacy socks and blue sandals and sat at the kitchen table, my legs swinging beneath me as I finished my favourite breakfast: sliced toast and a soft-boiled egg. I loved my soft-boiled eggs; it is how I still enjoy my eggs. I remember, many years later, how my mother commented on how surprised she was that I still enjoyed eggs after so long. Some things have never changed for me, and soft-boiled eggs in my diet have been a constant.

Sundays were a tradition where my father would call the house and take me out for the afternoon. On the approach to the afternoon, I felt an air of expectancy until the knock on the door came to pick me up. I felt extremely excited. My tummy had butterflies as I waited for my father to arrive and spend the afternoon with me. All I knew was that I was looking forward to riding alongside my dad in his car, wherever we went. The journey to Leverhulme Park was filled with a hum of anticipation. As we drove, I remember being in the passenger seat and feeling very special, as my father would play ska and reggae songs from the likes of Desmond Dekker and the Aces and tracks by them such as 'The Israelites', and 'Shanty Town' and Alton Ellis with 'Get Rock Steady'. The atmosphere had a high vibe, as we might say today, and I felt happy, safe, secure, loved, and cherished. The sun was high in the sky, and the park promised a day of fun and adventure.

We found a spot under a tree and my father laid out a blanket, and we settled down for the day. One of the first things he did was to take out his camera and, as I sat on the blanket, he snapped photo after photo, capturing smiles, my laughter, and the way the sunlight caught the bright red and gold ribbons in my hair. I remember feeling the centre of his attention and the subject of his artistry, but also slightly shy, as some people looked on at this little Black girl having lots of photos taken, which my father would send to my distant relatives who still lived in Jamaica who had never met me. The observers were not Black like my father.

I spent hours running from one activity to the next, my father close by, always ready with his camera. The swings were my favourite, with the feeling of soaring through the air exhilarating. My father pushed me higher and higher, and I squealed with delight. My hair didn't sway around if a sudden warm breeze should visit us in the park. The other girls were white, with different hair to mine. I loved my thick and long hair. I had "good hair" growing up in the tumultuous 60s, thick and curly, which stood out among my white friends even at 6 years old. I revelled in the uniqueness of my hair, embracing its beauty and texture. My hair and dark skin came from my ancestry, and I felt proud to shine my small light during this time.

The ice cream man was always there, dutifully serving parents who chose from a selection of ice creams, cornets, choc ices, lollies, torpedo wafers. I chose a 99 whipped ice cream with a chocolate flake in it and a lovely cool, fizzy drink of dandelion and burdock, my favourite drink. I felt a profound sense of gratitude for my mother, my dad, for Leverhulme Park, and for the beautiful fun memories that my dad and I created together on Sundays.

During this period, I played with my white friends without feeling any shadow of prejudice or the sting of exclusion. My mother and family nurtured my confidence against a backdrop of TV back then when only three channels were available. Apart from Floella Benjamin on BBC1 and, later, Sir Trevor Macdonald, who featured on *News at 10*. Positive role models through TV were rare. This lack of portrayal was beginning to program my mind that Black people were not good enough to feature on TV in a positive light, only to be denigrated on programmes such as *Love Thy Neighbour*. Comedy shows featured the likes of white male comedian Alf Garnett or the northern programme *The Comedians*, all highlighting Black people as a group to be laughed at and portrayed as second-class citizens.

My early educational formative years were spent at a humble primary school on a council estate, a time filled with joy and hardship, navigating the complexities of childhood in a white working-class school in the 60s. As Christmas approached, my school buzzed with anticipation for the nativity play. Every child eagerly awaited their role, hoping to be cast as a key character in the cherished British tradition. However, for a child like me, dreams of donning Mary's robes or angelic wings seemed far-fetched.

Instead, I found myself thrust into the background, assigned a role that felt more like a caricature than a character. Dressed in a grass skirt and adorned with coconuts around my neck, I was obvious among my peers and ridiculed, feeling second-class in my year, as opposed to the treatment of the majority white kids, including the very naughty kids. What truly set me apart was the mandate by the teacher to perform in the nativity play barefoot, which was a stark contrast to the shod feet of my classmates.

Feeling the chill of the wooden stage beneath my feet, I could not bear the discomfort any longer. Sneaking away, I slipped on my trusty black plimsolls, seeking solace in their familiar embrace, yet my moment of relief was shattered when the teacher looked at my feet and caught wind of my rebellion. With a voice that echoed across the hall, she berated me from the back of the hall for my audacity, accusing me of disrupting the sanctity of the nativity play, and I was slapped hard across my legs. The sting of the slap and her words cut deep, a painful reminder of my outside status in a world that seemed determined to keep me on the periphery, close but not too close, and constantly humiliated and ridiculed.

From that moment on, I retreated into the shadows, trying my best to avoid the spotlight at all costs. The sense of isolation weighed heavily on my young shoulders, a burden I struggled to bear. Yet, amid the darkness, a flicker of resilience ignited within me: I am just as good as my white school friends.

"Children should be seen and not heard," it was said. The alternative for the Black kid felt like: "Black kids must not be seen OR heard."

Traditional Western beauty standards often reflect European ideals, emphasising features such as straight hair, fair skin, and thin bodies. These ideals contrast sharply with Black beauty, which encompasses a diverse range of skin tones, hair textures, and body shapes. The prevalence of these beauty standards perpetuates colourism, a form of discrimination based on skin colour, seen within mainstream media and societal norms.

Growing up, the only Black woman reading the news on British TV channels was Moira Stewart. Floella Benjamin was my only 'go-to' for positive validation of Black women via British media, and they were both far lighter skinned than myself. Did this matter? As a child, seeing yourself reflected positively on the front cover of a girls' magazine or a glossy fashion magazine, or being able to access make-up for my skin colour, reaffirmed to me that dark-skinned Black women did not have a place in society apart from athletics or the music industry. White women were included and portrayed across every part of the media and sport. I could not see myself – and even my doll was white.

I had painful experiences of being bullied due to the colour of my skin while growing up. These experiences not only left me with emotional scars but also necessitated creative strategies to navigate everyday situations such as visiting the local corner shop without falling prey to the hostility of white girl gangs. The constant vigilance and adaptation required in such environments took a toll on my confidence and self-worth, shaping my early perceptions of identity and belonging. However, as my story unfolds, so does a journey of resilience and growth. Through introspection, support networks, and embracing my cultural heritage, I gradually reclaimed my confidence and sense of agency. This did not happen overnight, and my story delves into these transformative movements, illustrating how adversity can fuel development and empowerment, shaping a narrative of strength, resilience, and self-acceptance.

Growing up as a second-generation Black child I was constantly navigating between two distinct linguistic worlds. At home, the air was filled with the lively rhythm of Jamaican patois, a language that connected me to my cultural roots and gave our family a sense of unity. Outside, I encountered the thick northern Lancashire accent, shaped by the region's mining heritage, with its unique colloquialisms and clipped phrases. As a child, I became adept at switching between these languages, learning to decode the nuances of both, a skill that would serve me well as I moved through life.

But as my career progressed, particularly in corporate spaces where Black women were few and far between, I found myself again seeking the comfort of that familiar language. In white work environments, I would listen out for the subtle inflections of patois from Black colleagues whenever white co-workers were out of earshot. These moments of linguistic solidarity became a quiet form of resistance and a way to carve out our own psychological safety. Speaking patois in these settings was not just about communication — it was about creating a shared space where we could drop the mask, let off steam, and find comfort in each other's presence.

However, not all Black colleagues chose to engage in this code-switching within the workplace. Many felt the pressure to remain 'professional', adopting the language and mannerisms of the majority to fit in. This raised the question: if assimilating into the dominant culture set the tone for professionalism, where could Black colleagues truly feel safe?

I noticed a similar dynamic even when working in spaces like HMPs (Her Majesty's Prisons, as they were known at the time). Foreign prisoners would naturally gravitate toward each other, exercising and speaking in their native tongues, creating their own sense of community. Yet, despite being among others who looked like me, I often felt like I was on the periphery of their lives, held back by the weight of my own Superwoman cape. It was a reminder that the struggle to belong, to feel seen and understood, extends beyond just language — it is about finding spaces where you can show up fully as yourself, even when the environment pushes you to conform.

Yet, in that world of uncertainty, I found unexpected sources of hope and resilience — global icons who told me a different story about who I could be. Watching Muhammad Ali in interviews was nothing short of life-changing. Here was a Black man who boldly proclaimed "I am the greatest" with a level of self-belief that seemed almost impossible. His defiance and confidence pierced the doubts my imposter syndrome cape had woven into my psyche. Ali taught me that self-actualisation was not arrogance; it was a necessary act of survival and pride.

The West Indies cricket team led by Clive Lloyd also became a source of immense inspiration. Their historic victories over England were acts of triumph in a sport heavy with colonial legacy. Watching them play with such skill and grace, I felt a deep sense of vindication. It was a reminder that we, too, could be champions, that our excellence could shatter expectations. Their victories eased the weight of my imposter syndrome cape, whispering that our worth was undeniable.

Then there was the moment in 1976 when Miss Jamaica, Cindy Breakspeare, was crowned Miss World. In a society obsessed with Eurocentric beauty standards, seeing a Black woman celebrated for her beauty and grace was a revelation. It was a reminder that our features, our skin, our very essence, were worthy of admiration and celebration. These moments, these figures, soothed my soul, offering a counter-narrative to the constant sense of inadequacy I experienced on the ground.

The 1980s brought more role models in the form of Grace Jones and Joan Armatrading. Grace Jones shattered boundaries with her fearless androgyny and unapologetic presence. She defied every box society tried to put her in, standing tall and commanding attention. Joan Armatrading, with her soulful and introspective music, offered another kind of strength — one that acknowledged vulnerability but never let it define her worth. Their influence helped me start peeling away that imposter syndrome cape, thread by thread.

These global icons showed me that being Black was not just about enduring but about thriving, about embracing our strength and celebrating our uniqueness. They became my teachers in self-actualisation, empowering me to see my place in the world differently. They gave me the courage to start shedding that heavy cape, to let myself believe that I belonged, and to imagine a future where my voice, my dreams, and my joy mattered just as much as anyone else's.

In the 1960s, Caribbean immigrants in Britain often found themselves congregating at the same general practitioners (GPs) due to shared experiences of racial discrimination within the healthcare system. As a child, I remember the waiting room of our GP's surgery being consistently filled with Black patients, creating a space of familiarity amid an often-hostile environment. Our family doctor, Dr Meiring, an Irish physician, was known for his kindness and compassion, and he quickly became a trusted figure within the Caribbean community. His practice was one of the few where we felt seen and heard, in contrast to many other medical settings where Black patients faced overt discrimination or neglect. This was a time when structural racism was still deeply embedded in British society, even within its institutions, including the NHS. The Race Relations Act of 1965 — which was the first legislation to address racial discrimination — was limited in scope, focusing primarily on public places and lacking enforcement power. It was not until the Race Relations Act of 1968 that protection extended to housing, employment, and access to goods and services, including healthcare. However, even with these legal protections, unequal health outcomes persisted, as systemic biases in medical treatment were not easily dismantled by legislation alone.

Many Black patients continued to experience disparities in healthcare access, quality of treatment, and overall health outcomes, which were often overlooked by mainstream healthcare providers. Reports and studies from that era highlighted how Caribbean immigrants were disproportionately affected by conditions like hypertension, yet they were frequently misdiagnosed or undertreated due to racial biases in medical training and practice. The healthcare system, in many ways, upheld structural racism by perpetuating stereotypes and providing unequal care, even as new laws aimed to promote equal opportunities.

This era also brought the establishment of the NHS Reorganisation Act of 1973, which sought to unify health services but did little to address the racial disparities that affected Caribbean communities. The lack of culturally competent care and the presence of unconscious biases meant that many Black families continued to rely on the few doctors, like Dr Meiring, who treated them with dignity. As a result, word-of-mouth recommendations became crucial for finding sympathetic and understanding GPs. The crowded waiting rooms filled with faces like mine were a testament to the resilience of Caribbean immigrants, who found ways to navigate a healthcare system that was often indifferent or outright discriminatory, despite the legal frameworks intended to protect against such inequality.

Growing up in Bolton, I didn't always see reflections of myself in positions of power, leadership, or public influence. But, looking back now with a more conscious lens, I recognise there were indeed powerful role models within my own community – people whose very presence laid quiet but firm foundations for young Black girls like me to dream beyond what we could immediately see.

One such trailblazer was Campbell Jocelyn Hargreaves Benjamin, who made history as the first Black Mayor of Bolton, serving from 1993 to 1994. His leadership was not only symbolic but deeply impactful – a man who carried himself with dignity and dedication. In 1996, he was awarded an OBE for his unwavering service to the community. His contribution to civic life challenged the narratives too often imposed on Black men in Britain and offered a visible example of Black excellence rooted in community, service, and pride.

Another powerful presence was Clive Myrie, a fellow Boltonian, who would go on to become one of the most recognisable and respected journalists in the country. Seeing Clive deliver the national *News at 10* — that flagship, almost sacred British news bulletin — wasn't just about representation on screen. It was a moment of deep cultural significance. A Black man, from my town, was commanding the nation's attention with calm authority and journalistic rigour. He made it clear: we don't just deserve to be in the room — we belong at the front, leading the conversation.

At the time, I didn't have a long list of local role models who looked like me. But these two stood out — not just for what they achieved, but for how they carried themselves. Their presence became part of my internal compass, affirming that *possibility was not a distant hope — it was already happening*. They didn't just open doors; they held them open. And through their leadership example, a message whispered: *your time is coming.*

Reflecting on my lived experience as a child, I was acutely aware of the socio-economic challenges and disadvantages facing the Caribbean community in the 50s and 60s. This meant there were some significant barriers to accessing traditional banking services, and hence "Pardner" or "Sou Sou" was born.

Here are five reasons why the Pardner system was crucial in my community:

1. **Lack of Access to Banking**: Caribbean immigrants often faced discrimination from mainstream British banks, which were reluctant to offer loans, mortgages, or even basic accounts to Black customers. This made it difficult for them to save money, purchase property, or invest in their businesses.

2. **Community Support and Trust**: The Pardner system was built on trust within the community. It provided a way for members to support each other financially without relying on external institutions. The participants were usually friends, family members, or trusted members of the community, ensuring a level of accountability and trust that banks did not offer.

3. **Overcoming Economic Hardships**: For many immigrants, Pardner money was a lifeline that enabled them to overcome financial obstacles. The lump sum payouts could be used for a variety of purposes, such as:

    - Paying off debts
    - Setting up small businesses
    - Paying rent or deposits for housing
    - Covering unexpected expenses or sending money back home to the Caribbean

4. **Financial Empowerment**: Pardner allowed members to save money in a disciplined way, offering a sense of financial independence. In an era where credit options were limited and often predatory, this system gave Caribbean immigrants an alternative way to manage their finances.

Social Solidarity: Beyond its financial benefits, Pardner fostered a sense of community and solidarity among Caribbean immigrants. It was a way to stay connected and support one another in a foreign and often-hostile environment.

Impact on the Community

The Pardner system played a significant role in helping Caribbean immigrants establish themselves in Britain. It allowed many to save up for important investments like buying their first homes or starting their own businesses. The collective savings model also helped to maintain cultural ties and promote mutual support, acting as a social safety net in times of financial difficulty.

For me, Pardner money was more than just an informal savings scheme; it was a testament to the resilience and ingenuity of Caribbean immigrants in Britain. By leveraging communal trust and support, they created a financial system that allowed them to thrive despite the challenges of discrimination and exclusion from mainstream financial institutions. Today, the Pardner concept still exists in various forms across Caribbean and African communities in the UK and beyond, continuing to serve as a vital source of economic empowerment.

When I was growing up, there was always someone in the community with an allotment. On weekends, I remember an uncle from the neighbourhood showing up with a bounty of fresh produce — carrots, cabbage, callaloo, or potatoes — straight from his patch of land. Sharing food like this was a hallmark of our local Caribbean community, a way of looking out for one another. There was also always someone with a barbershop set up in their garage. Black men from the area would gather there for a fresh trim. The barber, a true Jamaican elder, had a reliable set of clippers and a warm, welcoming vibe. The air buzzed with chatter, reggae music, and the scent of fresh clippings — it was a cultural hub.

Weekends were also steeped in culinary traditions. Saturday was all about Jamaican soup, a hearty, soul-warming dish packed with yams, dumplings, pumpkin, and meats like chicken or beef. This was not just a meal; it was a Jamaican ritual, filling bellies and bringing people together. Sunday dinner was sacred too, centred around the iconic chicken, rice, and peas. And yes, it is *rice and peas* — never *peas and rice*! It still makes me chuckle when non-Jamaicans mix it up. There is an order to the name of this dish, and it is as serious as the care we take in preparing it.

Easter held its own special traditions. Back then, there was a Jamaican bakery in Moss Side, Manchester, which was the go-to spot for all things Jamaican breads and treats. One of the Jamaicans where we all lived who had a car would bring back patties — flaky, golden pastries filled with spicy meat or vegetables. As a child, I did not appreciate them; they were far too fiery for my Lancashire-influenced palate. But as I grew older, I developed a love for their bold, complex flavours and can never get enough of them and believe that I am a bit of an 'aficionado' in the British Jamaican patties space! Of course, Easter was not complete without bun and cheese. Jamaican bun — a sweet, spiced loaf packed with dried fruits — and cheddar cheese was the de-rigueur pairing.

The tradition of bun and cheese at Easter has its roots in Jamaica's colonial history, inspired by British hot cross buns, a Lenten staple. Over time, Jamaicans made their own, replacing the cross with dried fruits, spices, and molasses for extra richness. Paired with salty cheese, the combination became a cherished Easter delicacy for us. These meals were not just about food; they were about connection, culture, and passing down traditions that bridged generations Certainly, second-generation Jamaicans would understand what was meant by bun and cheese.

The anticipation of Christmas was tied as much to the food as to the festivities. One of the most iconic symbols of the season was the Jamaican Christmas cake, or black cake. My mother is an excellent cook and cake maker and, months before December, I would see large glass jars tucked away in the cupboard, filled with a mysterious, dark, rich mixture of fruits — raisins, prunes, currants, and cherries — soaking in a potent bath of rum and red wine. The aroma was intoxicating, even as a child. It was a heady mix of sweetness and spice that hinted that Christmas, and indulgence, was to come. The jars were opened occasionally by my mother, who would add more rum to ensure the fruits remained deeply steeped, soft, and bursting with flavour.

Christmas dinner was always a feast of Jamaican culinary pride, highlighting dishes steeped in heritage. The Christmas table was vibrant with options, reflecting the richness of Jamaican culture. Alongside the Western staples like roast turkey or chicken, we also had:

- **Callaloo**: A leafy green dish cooked down with onions, tomatoes, garlic, and sometimes salted cod for added flavour.

- **Ackee and Saltfish**: Jamaica's national dish, where the buttery ackee fruit was sautéed with salted cod, onions, and scotch bonnet peppers, adding a spicy kick.

- **Fried Dumplings**: Crispy on the outside and soft on the inside, they were perfect for scooping up gravy or enjoying on their own.

- **Rice and Peas**: Made with coconut milk and flavoured with thyme and scallions, this was a staple of every celebration.

- **Sorrel Drink**: A tangy, ruby-red drink made from the petals of the sorrel plant, steeped with ginger, cloves, and cinnamon, and sweetened to taste. It was often laced with rum for the adults.

In the run up to Christmas in our house, the kitchen was always a hub of activity, with the clatter of the Dutch pot as it hit the stove or as food was fried or sealed. Every Jamaican home that I knew of and visited had a Dutch pot, which was a staple of cooking equipment and has cultural significance to its origins and its presence in Jamaican homes. The Dutch pot's presence in Jamaica reflects the influence of Dutch colonists who introduced cast-iron cookware to the Caribbean during the colonial era. Over time, Jamaicans adapted the Dutch pot their culinary traditions. It became integral to preparing our iconic dishes. These meals were more than just food; they were a connection to our Jamaican roots, a celebration of family, and a comforting reminder of home.

70s Racial Violence on the Streets Up North.

Before stepping into the world of leadership, before I even had the language to name concepts like imposter syndrome, I had already learned how to navigate spaces where I was made to feel I didn't belong. This chapter delves into the early years of my life, where survival meant strategy, and awareness meant safety.

Trigger Warning:

This section contains references to racism and physical violence. My intention in sharing this is not to dwell on trauma but to illustrate how these experiences shaped my leadership mindset, resilience, and ability to navigate environments not built for my success. For many women of colour, imposter syndrome is not simply about self-doubt — it is reinforced by systems and experiences that tell us, from an early age, that we do not belong. This is my story of how I learned to see, strategise, and survive — skills that later equipped me to lead.

I am no stranger to violence, but I have never worn the label of victim. From an early age, I learned to be watchful, always attuned to my surroundings. Hypervigilance was not something I acquired as a leader — it was instilled in me as a child. I had to read people, anticipate threats, and calculate risks before I even understood what those words meant.

Growing up on a Lancashire council estate, my family was one of only two Black households on our street. That difference made us visible. It also made us targets. Racist gangs lurked in the alleyways and near the shops, and I knew that a routine errand for my mother could turn into a chase, a confrontation, or worse. There were no safe shortcuts — only calculated decisions on which route might expose me to the least danger.

I became an expert in strategic thinking and masking long before I had the words for it — learning when to blend in, when to stand my ground, and when to walk away. I could sense hostility before it erupted, anticipate the shift in body language before the first insult was thrown. Even the dogs were weaponised, set upon me by the kids who laughed as I ran or just froze to the spot. But running wasn't about fear — it was about preservation.

At the time, I didn't connect these experiences to leadership. I didn't recognise that I was building a skill set that would later allow me to navigate boardrooms, manage conflicts, and maintain my composure in spaces where I wasn't always welcomed. I learned early how to read an environment, how to respond rather than react, and how to keep moving forward — even when I wasn't supposed to succeed.

Looking back, it is no surprise that I later pursued a career in social justice. Without realising it, I had already been preparing for it. The world had shown me how injustice operated first-hand, and rather than being broken by it, I turned that awareness into action.

These experiences planted the seeds of my resilience — but they also planted something else: the quiet, creeping feeling that I was always being watched, always being judged, always one step away from having to prove myself. This is where imposter syndrome often begins — not as a whisper of self-doubt, but as an external force telling us we do not belong.

Yet, from those early years, I gained more than just wounds — I gained wisdom. And that wisdom would carry me into leadership, shaping the way I moved through a world that tried to tell me I had no place.

First Speck: A Rite of Passage and a New Responsibility

I was fourteen years old when it happened — a single, surprising speck of blood that marked the transition from childhood to something I could not yet fully comprehend. It was a quiet, unassuming morning, the kind where nothing extraordinary seems possible. I remember the sense of confusion, the slight twinge of embarrassment, even though I was alone. But there was a strange, almost electric thrill that coursed through me. This was it. The moment that my biology teacher had hinted at in clinical, sanitised terms: *menstruation*.

I found my mother almost immediately. I was nervous, and unsure of what to say. I was not exactly afraid, but there was a heaviness, a shift in the air between us as I stammered out my discovery. To my surprise, she did not look shocked or even mildly surprised. She simply nodded, her face softening into a smile that spoke of a knowing far beyond my limited understanding. Without a word, she led me to her bedroom, and I watched as she reached for something hidden away on the top of her wardrobe.

Out came a pack of Dr Whites — huge, heavy pads that were more like nappies than the slim, disposable ones we take for granted today. I remember staring at them, wide-eyed, trying to reconcile the odd contraption with the fact that this was now a part of my life. These pads had hooks on either end, designed to attach to a belt. And, sure enough, my mother handed me one of those belts, the elastic band that would wrap around my waist and anchor the bulky pad in place.

There was no ceremony, no lengthy talk about womanhood or the mysteries of life. My mother simply showed me how to hook the pad into the belt with the ease of someone who had done this many times before, as though it was the most natural thing in the world. In that moment, I felt a surge of pride and an odd kind of excitement. I was part of a lineage of women who had come before me, all managing this secret, sacred rite of passage.

But with that newfound sense of maturity came a sudden, sobering thought: I was no longer a child. The lessons from my biology class came flooding back — diagrams of ovaries and fallopian tubes, the clinical talk of eggs and cycles. Technically, I realised, I could get pregnant now. It was a strange, jarring realisation, like a door had been opened into a world I was not sure I was ready to enter. I felt empowered and burdened, like I was carrying something precious and fragile, something that could change my life in ways I could not yet imagine.

I felt grown up in a way that I was not entirely ready for, teetering on the edge between childhood innocence and the complexities of womanhood. My mother's quiet preparation — her stash of Dr Whites, the ease with which she handed me the belt — was like a baton being passed. It was a signal that I was stepping into a new phase of life, one that she had prepared me for in ways I had not even realised.

I write about this day because it marks an important phase of my life, a journey I would later transpose out of as I moved into menopause. It is a full circle, from the initiation of menstruation to the concluding chapter of it. The symbolism of my first period, and the rituals that came with it, have stayed with me throughout my life. They shaped my understanding of what it means to be a woman in a world that often expects us to carry more than our fair share of burdens, whether we are ready or not.

I could not help but think, even then, how different this moment might have been if I had grown up somewhere else. In Europe, where I was raised, the onset of menstruation was treated with a kind of quiet practicality. My mother had everything meticulously organised – the Dr Whites, the belt, the silent handover of knowledge – like it was simply another task to be managed. There were no celebrations, no special ceremonies, just a nod to growing up and the tools to manage it.

But I was aware, even as a young girl, that this was not the case everywhere. In other parts of the world, a girl's first period is celebrated with joy, pride, and by the community. In some cultures, it is a time of festivity. In parts of India, for example, girls are adorned with new clothes and jewellery, their families throwing grand celebrations to mark their entrance into womanhood. In Ghana, a girl's first menstruation is an occasion to be celebrated with the Dipo ceremony, a rite of passage where girls are honoured and their transition into adulthood is recognised with song, dance, and blessings from elders. Across Latin America, it is common for girls to receive gifts, cakes, or even small parties – moments of joy shared with loved ones.

I wondered what it would be like to have this milestone treated as something triumphant rather than as something to keep discreet. In stark contrast to these vibrant celebrations, my experience was muted, a private matter to be managed behind closed doors. It was a reminder that in Europe, menstruation is often seen as something to manage quietly, as though it were something to be ashamed of, rather than a natural and powerful sign of growth.

Reflecting on this, I realise that my own journey with my body was shaped by this subdued, almost clinical introduction to menstruation. It became something I had to manage alone, with resilience and quiet strength, rather than something to be proud of or to share. This difference in how the first period is marked speaks volumes about how society views women and their bodies – a message that stayed with me as I moved through the various phases of womanhood.

For me, that moment at fourteen was the beginning of a lifelong journey of reconciling what it means to carry the weight of womanhood in a world that often fails to celebrate the very things that make us powerful.

Attending an all-girls school added an extra layer of complexity to my journey into womanhood. I was often ridiculed, particularly during gym class. Back in those days, we were made to wear gym knickers – those short, revealing bottoms that offered little in the way of comfort or modesty. Unless, of course, you were on your period. Then, you had the privilege of reporting to the gym teacher, explaining why you could not participate fully, why you could not shower with everyone else, and why you needed to be excused from certain activities. I can still remember the humiliating walk to the teacher's desk, the whispers and smirks from classmates who knew exactly why you were stepping forward.

What should have been a time of joy and discovery became a period of shame and anxiety, especially for me as the only Black girl in the class. The isolation I felt during those years was not just about being different in appearance; it was about the layers of cultural stigma that came with being the 'other'. There was no one else who looked like me, who understood the awkwardness of dealing with periods, bras, and all the changes that come with growing up. It felt like I was navigating a minefield of insecurities, with the added pressure of trying to fit into a space that was never quite designed for me.

Yet, there were moments of joy, too. Once I overcame the stigma of periods and bras — those initial hurdles that made me feel so different — I began to find my stride. The best times were when we played hockey on the fields that separated our school from the all-boys school next door. There was a thrill in those games, a kind of freedom in racing across the grass, the boys' laughter and cheers drifting over from the other side. It was during those moments that I felt most alive, most connected to the strength of my body, rather than ashamed of it.

Those school years, despite the challenges, ended up being some of the best times of my life. I found resilience in the small victories — overcoming the embarrassment of wearing a bra for the first time, surviving the whispered jokes about periods, and finding my own ways to navigate the unspoken rules of girlhood. What started as a journey fraught with shame slowly transformed into a discovery of my own strength, a recognition that being different was not a weakness but a source of power.

But I cannot help thinking how different it could have been if my first period had been celebrated, if there had been pride instead of ridicule, support instead of whispers. It is a reminder of how deeply the messages we receive about our bodies can shape us, and how important it is to rewrite those narratives — for ourselves and for the girls who come after us.

Shades of Trouble and Unrest:

Growing up as a Black teenager in the north-west of England during the 70s and 80s was a time of immense turmoil and tension. The riots that erupted involving Black youths were a response to the pervasive racial discrimination and harassment we faced daily. The notorious 'sus laws' allowed police to stop and search Black individuals based on mere suspicion, leading to countless humiliating encounters that fuelled anger and resentment within our community. The tension between Black communities and the authorities was palpable, with the constant fear of being unjustly targeted. For a teenage Black girl like me, the impact was profound.

Music played a pivotal role in providing solace and fostering a sense of solidarity during these challenging times. The reggae anthem 'Police and Thieves' by Junior Murvin resonated deeply, as it echoed our frustrations and defiance. The music scene, particularly the rise of Northern soul, became a sanctuary where the lines of 'us' and 'them' blurred, and unity thrived. Northern soul, a genre rooted in Black American soul music, brought together Black and white northerners in a shared appreciation of its infectious rhythms and dance culture.

Every weekend, I would travel to the mecca of the north-west for music — Wigan. Wigan Casino, the Wigan Pier, and the jazz funk club Casinelli's where dancing was my weekly escape, I would dance my weekends away to the sounds of jazz, funk, and soul. The experience was not just about the music; it was a form of restorative healing. It provided a sense of belonging and connection that, through music, transcended racial boundaries. Lifelong friendships were forged on those dance floors, friendships that have endured despite my relocation from the north-west.

Throughout my career, I have come to understand that white supremacy is not confined to overt ideology. It is embedded deep within the systems, structures, and everyday assumptions that shape our professional worlds. It seeps into policy, culture, and expectation — often unnoticed by those who benefit from its design. But for Black women, its presence is keenly felt.

One of the most visible — and yet persistently denied — battlegrounds of this systemic bias is Black hair. I have seen, time and again, how workplace norms are shaped by Eurocentric definitions of what is "professional," "neat," or "appropriate." These unspoken codes often favour straightened or chemically altered hair, subtly reinforcing the notion that our natural textures, braids, locs, and protective styles are somehow less than — unkempt, unprofessional, even rebellious.

This isn't just about style. It's about identity. It's about belonging.

The scrutiny and policing of Black hair in professional spaces is not incidental; it is symptomatic of a wider discomfort with our presence — a quiet demand that we shrink ourselves to fit into spaces never designed with us in mind.

Research from Dove UK's CROWN Fund affirms what so many of us already know from lived experience: Black women in Britain are disproportionately likely to face discrimination, microaggressions, and exclusion based on our hair. Behind these statistics are stories of girls sent home from school, women passed over for promotion, and leaders — like myself — who have had to navigate complex decisions about how we show up in rooms of power.

Our hair is not the problem. The problem lies in the systems that view our authenticity as a threat.

This chapter marks the beginning of an honest exploration. Not just of my professional journey – but of what it means to lead while Black, while woman, while true to oneself. It is about shedding the cape of assimilation and daring to stand in the fullness of who we are.

Let us begin by unravelling the strands – of power, of pain, and of possibility.

*Create a text box for this activity

> **Reflective Prompt for the Black and Brown Woman of Colour**
>
> "In what ways have you felt pressure to conform to unspoken rules of professionalism that did not honour your identity, including how you wear your hair or present yourself? What choices have you made to protect or express your authentic self, and how did those choices impact your sense of belonging, safety, or power?"
>
> 📝 *Use this space to reclaim your narrative. Reflect on how these moments shaped your leadership journey, and consider what liberation looks like for you now.*

*Create a text box for this activity

> **Reflective Prompt for Black woman Ally**
>
> "When have you witnessed standards of professionalism marginalising Black and Brown colleagues, particularly around hair or appearance? How did you respond—or not respond—and what

can you commit to doing differently to challenge bias and create truly inclusive spaces?"

📝 *Reflect honestly. Allyship is not a label—it is a continuous, visible practice. Consider one meaningful action you can take this week to stand in solidarity.*

Music for me has been a source of comfort and unity. It offered moments of escape and connection, a rhythm to hold onto when the world felt uncertain. Yet, even as the music played and lifted my spirit, the deeper realities of being a Black girl growing up in Britain could not be drowned out.

Beneath the melodies, a quieter, more insidious rhythm pulsed—one of hypervigilance. The kind that seeps in early, shaped by unspoken fears and visible threats. This ever-present state of alertness became the backdrop to my life, following me into adulthood and my working life. It eventually manifested as anxiety, stress, and health challenges—particularly during menopause, a life phase where I observed many Black women silently carry the compounded weight of it all. This state of constant alertness and hypervigilance took a toll on my health and well-being, contributing to chronic conditions which are mostly prevalent among Black women coming to the fore during menopause when we are stripped of particular hormones that would normally have carried us through.

Music was, and still is, a restorative way of healing a cultural force throughout my life, from the ska tunes that filled my family home to the Northern soul anthems that fuelled my adolescence, and the sounds of northern funk from 80's bands such as the Liverpool Black band The Real Thing helped to create balance.

Growing Up in Turmoil: Race, Resilience, and the Politics of Survival in 1970s Britain

Enoch Powell, a British Conservative politician, is a notable figure in this context. Powell served as an MP and held various positions, including Minister of Health and Shadow Secretary of State for Defence. He is best known for his controversial "rivers of blood" speech in 1968, where he criticised immigration from the New Commonwealth and opposed anti-discrimination legislation. Powell's rhetoric and policies contributed to a climate of racial tension and division, which has had lasting impacts on how Black individuals, including post-menopausal women, are perceived, and treated in British society.

Authoring this book as a Black woman, I cannot separate the Black woman narrative from the political, as the very label 'Black' carries inescapable political connotations. Every public document I complete — whether as a patient, an employee, or a victim of crime — requires my race to be accounted for, a constant reminder of the systemic structures that seek to define and classify me. Growing up in Lancashire during the 1970s — a time of immense social and economic turbulence — I witnessed first-hand the unravelling of working-class livelihoods. I was among the last children to receive free school milk before it was abolished in 1971 under Margaret Thatcher's education reforms, a policy that signalled the tightening grip of austerity. The bread strikes, electricity blackouts, and widespread industrial action brought the region to its knees, especially in the cotton mills, which were the backbone of the local economy.

The collapse of the cotton industry hit working-class communities hard, but its impact on Black and minority ethnic workers was particularly acute. Many Black families had been recruited to work in these industries during the post-war years, filling roles that white workers often avoided. With the mills closing, these workers faced compounded challenges: not only joblessness but systemic racism in securing new employment. Black workers were often the first to be laid off and the last to be rehired, deepening racial inequities. I remember hearing about fathers and uncles queuing for jobs, only to be turned away because of the colour of their skin, while others faced openly discriminatory hiring practices.

Beyond the economic struggles, the racial climate of the 1970s was fraught with tension. The *Sus* laws – stop-and-search powers disproportionately used against Black youths – fuelled distrust and fear within our communities. Stories of friends or neighbours being targeted and harassed by police were commonplace. These experiences left scars on the collective psyche of Black communities, fostering a sense of anger and an urgent need for solidarity. Amid this turmoil, music became a powerful outlet for expression and resistance. Anti-racism anthems like The Specials' 'Ghost Town' captured the despair and resilience of the time, their lyrics mirroring the crumbling streets and fractured opportunities I saw around me. I was drawn to this music – it spoke to my experiences and gave voice to the frustrations of a generation grappling with systemic inequities.

These experiences shaped me profoundly. I saw both the harsh realities of racism and the resilience of community solidarity. Neighbours, regardless of background, often pulled together to support one another in the face of strikes, shortages, and social unrest. This sense of collective strength and shared struggle stood in stark contrast to the more individualistic ethos I would later observe in the south of England. These formative years taught me the value of unity in adversity and planted the seeds for my lifelong dedication to diversity, equality, and inclusion. My attraction to working within the social realm – addressing systemic injustice and amplifying marginalised voices — stems directly from these early experiences. They are a reminder of how interconnected our struggles are and of the power we hold when we come together.

Little Beverley

Beverley A. Powell - age 6 years old

Chapter 2
UNDER THE SUPERWOMAN CAPE

British Education Part 1 - Primary School

"We don't like Niggers here"

Schooled by the System, Raised by Truth

Before the 1976 Race Relations Act even whispered of equality, I was already immersed in a system that told me I was less than. British schooling in those years wasn't neutral — it was an extension of empire, designed not to educate but to erase, to diminish, to make us feel grateful for inclusion while keeping us invisible.

I still remember sitting in class history lesson as a teacher described Africa as a land of "savages" civilised by British missionaries. Those words cut deep. There was no mention of Mali, Songhai, African scholars or revolutionaries — just a narrative that painted my people as primitive and our history as irrelevant. This wasn't ignorance; it was systemic racism, delivered with the authority of education.

At home my Jamaican parents — alert, aware — taught us differently. They told us stories, shared our true history, and reminded us that we mattered. It wasn't formal education, but it planted seeds strong enough to help us remember that we came from somewhere significant. Still, for a child, holding two truths — the violence of school and the clarity of home — was confusing and heavy.

Then, in 1977, *Roots* was aired on BBC1. The novel written by Alex Haley on the saga of an America family was first aired on ABC in January 1977 in the US. For many, it was a cultural moment. For me, it was personal. My auntie's mother's sister bought the book and sent it from the US. Reading it shook me. It laid bare the brutality and resilience of our history. But it was the response at school that cut deepest. White classmates began mocking me, calling me "Kizzy". It wasn't affection — it was ridicule. I shrank. I didn't yet have the words or the fire. I just knew I hated it.

I became the quiet Black girl in the background — unseen, unsure, trying not to take up space. The system had worked. Just as Malcolm X said: "If you stick a knife in my back nine inches and pull it out six inches, there's no progress..."

I had a backdoor mindset. I didn't believe I deserved the spotlight or the mic. That kind of reprogramming took years, decades. I only began unlearning the damage when my career forced me to confront the internal limits I'd absorbed. When leadership called, I had to choose: stay silent in the back or step forward and rise.

I wasn't just educated by the system — I was conditioned by it. Reclaiming myself demanded truth, rage, and healing in equal measure.

"If I didn't define myself, I would be crunched into other people's fantasies for me and eaten alive." — *Audre Lorde*

In primary school, every Monday we registered for class and paid dinner money. I was the only Black child — and the only one receiving free school meals. That difference marked me. Week after week, I was publicly singled out with taunts like, "Why should she get free dinners, Miss?" The humiliation was relentless. Even though I knew other children also received support, the spotlight always found me. That ritual etched shame into my sense of self-worth.

Those moments shaped me. They didn't just teach me about poverty — they taught me how the system assigns value. But they also sowed the roots of compassion. During school holidays, when families like mine received free meals for the full six weeks, I began to understand struggle not just as something to survive, but as something that connects. That understanding still fuels my advocacy and leadership today.

Back at school during this period, the "eleven-plus" exam loomed large — a national test that determined which children could attend grammar school. I did not pass. At the time, I felt crushed, as though I had failed a test of my worth. Reflecting on it years later, I noticed a pattern: a high percentage of those who passed at my school did not seem to excel in later life, while many of their parents were actively involved as school governors or committee members. It made me question the fairness of the system and whether it truly measured potential or reinforced privilege.

In my academic studies later in my years, I gained a deeper and more nuanced understanding of intelligence and childhood development and trauma, which reshaped my perspective on intelligence. Intelligence is not fixed, especially at the age of eleven; it is fluid, multifaceted, and influenced by a child's environment, experiences, and opportunities. My research in child psychology highlights that children develop at different rates and often show strengths in ways traditional tests like the eleven-plus fail to capture. This realisation helped me see my own journey differently, recognising that my path to academic and professional success was not defined by one early setback, but by a broader, lifelong process of learning and growth.

Early Leadership Lessons from a Black Girlhood:
1. **Visibility is power**
   The early experience of being silenced or sidelined taught me the cost of invisibility. Leadership begins with stepping forward — claiming space, voice, and truth, especially when systems are designed to erase you.

2. **Lived experience is expertise**
   My story — rooted in race, class, and survival — became a source of authority. It gave me insight, empathy, and a deep

commitment to equity that no textbook could teach. Effective leadership isn't just about credentials — it's about consciousness.

3. **Rewriting the narrative is transformational**
Understanding that intelligence is not fixed helped me shift from shame to strength. Leaders must challenge fixed definitions — of worth, of success, of ability. My journey taught me that redefining potential begins with unlearning the stories we were told about ourselves.

Secondary School

My secondary school held great memories for me and some of my happiest memories. I attended an all-girls school, Castle Hill High School for Girls, Bolton. I remember how excited I was in my brand-spanking uniform which was green, with a green and gold tie. My name was called out along with other newbies. We were asked to form a line, where we were then asked to follow the teacher to our classroom. I recall being the only Black girl in the class. I stood at the end of the line.

A tall white girl with red hair and freckles came from the front of the queue towards me and said: "We don't like niggers here." I felt bewildered and shocked on my very first day. What an introduction to big school! Clearly this girl had assumed role of class spokesperson and decreed that none of the class liked Black kids. This was not the case and, in fact, as I write my story, those girls from that class remain lifelong friends.

At secondary school, the phrase I heard most often from teachers — particularly my white teachers — was that I had an *attitude*. It did not seem to matter that I was an A-student, that I showed up, did the work, and did it well. The word *attitude* was never about my academic performance. It was about how I carried myself. How I spoke with confidence. How I held my own space.

Looking back, I see now that what they really meant was that I did not shrink.

Those comments could have broken my spirit, but instead, they fuelled something deeper in me. Over time, I developed what I now understand to be an *inner locus of control*. I began to realise that I could not always change how others saw me, but I could choose how I saw myself. And I credit a big part of that to my mother. Even from back home, her voice was strong in my ears: "You are good enough — just as you are." She helped build my foundation. Her belief in me helped shape my own.

As I grew into myself, so did my sense of style. I have always been drawn to bold colours, bright beads, statement earrings — pieces that speak before I do. I did not realise it at the time, but I was cultivating a personal brand rooted in identity and heritage. There was something powerful, almost ancestral, in my pull toward reds, oranges, and rich earth tones. It was a quiet nod to the strength of my African roots.

It is interesting, then, that my career took me into worlds defined by structure and uniformity — spaces like the police, the prison service, the NHS — where regulation and dark colours were the norm. They are environments where blending in was often easier than standing out. Yet even in those spaces, my style remained a small rebellion, a quiet reminder to myself of who I was and where I came from. I learned to adapt without erasing myself.

But in my later years, I began to reflect more deeply and honestly. I started to see the ways I had unknowingly worn the Superwoman cape — always competent, always composed, always the fixer. I realised how often I had dampened my own light in the name of professionalism. I was showing up, yes – but sometimes hidden. I was hidden behind uniforms, behind expectations, behind the need to be beyond reproach.

It was a survival tactic; one many Black women know all too well. But it came at a cost. And so, part of my personal reclamation has been learning to take off that cape, to let myself be seen – not just for what I can *do*, but for who I *am*, to honour the fullness of my identity, and to wear my brightness boldly, in every sense of the word.

One of the opportunities I took up while in secondary school was volunteering at a local women's refuge centre in Bolton. I helped with organising activities for children and supporting day-to-day tasks, which taught me empathy, active listening, and how to hold space for others in vulnerable situations. These skills stayed with me and became the foundation for my future career in supporting others. More personally, I could never have predicted that, years later, I would draw on that same strength and understanding when I faced shame and fear from violence in my own relationship.

As a young Black girl growing up in an environment of direct confrontational hostility in the 60s and 70s, there was a distinct lack of representation and recognition of their beauty in mainstream media and popular culture. It had a profound effect on my self-esteem and sense of identity. The limited portrayal of Black women, especially the older Black women, as role models in positions of power and influence, exacerbates this issue. Without positive representation of myself, I struggled to envision myself achieving full potential. The impact of colourism extended beyond beauty standards to affect various aspects of life, including education, employment, and interpersonal relationships.

Drawing strength from my ancestors, I vowed to rise above the prejudice and direct discrimination that threatened to hold me back. Clad in my imaginary Superwoman cape of courage, I faced each new school day with determination, knowing I had to work twice as hard as my white peers to be treated the "same as", as I was told numerous times by my mother.

Journaling Prompt:

Double the Struggle

Growing up on a council estate, I quickly learned that opportunities were not handed to you on a silver platter. There was no 'old money' to rely on. Old money refers to wealth that has been inherited over generations rather than earned within a single lifetime. Families with old money often have a long history of wealth and social status, and their assets are passed down through the family line. This kind of wealth can provide significant social and economic advantages, and, for me, there was no old money that could cushion me from a grandma or grandad if I wanted to go straight from school to university. Grandad and Grandmother were busy building firm family foundations in Lancashire to support my mother and father as the next generation arrived to work in Britain and help to build up the country after World War II.

Many significant sacrifices were made by the Caribbean community with the promise of being supported by the mother land as our relatives and now ancestors arrived on ships such as the *Empire Windrush* to support Britain after the war. Growing up, it was disheartening to see my school history lessons overlook the rich tapestry of my ancestry and the critical contributions of Black people to World War II, which were pivotal in Britain's victory. Instead, the curriculum painted a skewed picture, portraying Africans as savages tamed by missionaries. This narrative left a lasting imprint on my psyche, shaping my understanding of the impact of having Black skin and the importance of recognising and celebrating our true history.

For a Black family that emigrated from Jamaica to Britain, the concept of old money was particularly relevant. We had no history of inherited wealth and therefore we were disadvantaged not only due to the colour of our skin but also the social and economic disadvantages that came with it. This meant fewer opportunities for education, employment, and social mobility along with the layer of systemic racism which I have already highlighted.

Growing up in Lancashire, a painful reminder of my ancestry was knowing that my ancestors' money was tied up in buildings and land in the county previously owned by slave owners, which meant that the wealth accumulated through slavery has been passed down through generations and is still present in the form of property and land. It is a painful reminder of the injustices of the past and the ongoing impact of slavery on present-day Black people.

Examples of Historical Slave Owners in Lancashire:

Lancashire, particularly Lancaster, was heavily involved in the transatlantic slave trade. Some notable historical figures include:

- **Abraham Rawlinson (1738-1803)**: An MP for Lancaster who participated in the slave trade.

- **Charles Inman (1725-1767)**: A commissioner for the Lancaster Port Commission.

- **Thomas Hinde (1720-1798)**: Twice Mayor of Lancaster.

Land and Buildings in Manchester or Lancashire Owned by Ancestors' Slave Owners

Many buildings and pieces of land in Manchester and Lancashire were financed by profits from slavery. For example, some of the grand houses and estates in the area were built with wealth accumulated through the slave trade. These properties often bear the names of their original owners, serving as a reminder of their history.

Northern Soul Music

Northern soul is a cultural phenomenon rooted in the industrial towns of northern England, a paradox of geography and origin. The term was coined in the early 1970s by journalist Dave Godin, who used it to describe the enthusiastic embrace of obscure American soul records by working-class northern communities. Yet, this music, born in the sweat-drenched clubs of places like Wigan Casino and Blackpool Mecca, was forged thousands of miles away in the United States. Despite its northern English moniker, the origins of Northern soul are deeply intertwined with the migration and struggles of Black artists in the United States, many of whom sought refuge and opportunity in the northern cities of America to escape the stifling racial oppression of the South.

Motown — a cornerstone of this movement — emerged from Detroit, Michigan, under the guidance of Berry Gordy. Known as the 'Motown Sound', it fused infectious rhythms with poignant melodies, aiming to transcend racial boundaries and appeal to a broad audience. Yet, this success did not shield Black artists from systemic discrimination. Many performers, including Marvin Gaye, Martha Reeves, and The Temptations, faced barriers that necessitated relocating to Detroit or Chicago, hubs where burgeoning record labels like Tamla Motown and Chess Records gave Black musicians the tools to share their voices. Among these artists, Marvin Gaye's contributions stand out not only for their musical brilliance but for their enduring socio-political resonance. His 1971 album *What's Going On* is often hailed as one of the most influential recordings in soul music history, seamlessly blending Motown aesthetics with a sharp critique of societal issues.

Growing up in the north of England, music was everywhere — it was not just entertainment; it was a lifeline. For working-class Black women like me, Northern soul scene brought something special. It was a world where you could lose yourself in the beats, spin on the dance floor, and feel free, even for just one night. But the music we loved — those fast, upbeat tracks from American Black artists — did not start here. It came from across the Atlantic, born out of the struggles of Black musicians in the US, many of whom moved to northern cities like Detroit or Chicago to escape the oppression of the South.

Northern soul was not just about music; it was about finding joy in unlikely places. Clubs like Wigan Casino were packed with dancers moving to Motown tracks that were not big hits back in America but became iconic here. Marvin Gaye, Martha Reeves, The Temptations — they were stars in our eyes, even if they were overlooked in their own country. Marvin Gaye stood out. His music spoke to the soul, but it also spoke to the struggles we knew too well, whether it was about love, loss, or standing up against injustice.

Fashion played a big part, too. You could not move like that on the dance floor without the right clothes. For women, it was all about flared skirts and sleeveless tops — easy to dance in but still stylish. For men, sharp trousers and bowling shirts were the norm. And unlike the rave scene that came later, Northern soul was not about drugs. We were high on the music and the movement — it was pure energy and passion.

By the 1990s, Manchester's rave scene was making waves, but it was a quite different vibe. Clubs like the Hacienda brought in electronic beats, and bands like the Happy Mondays and The Stone Roses dominated the scene. While it was exciting, you did not see many Black groups in that space. For us, the reggae scene ran parallel, rooted in the Caribbean communities of Moss Side and Hulme. The sound systems and dancehall culture there were our thing – a connection to home and heritage.

And then there was cricket. If music was life, cricket was religion in many Black Caribbean households, mine included. My grandad was obsessed. When the West Indies played, the entire world stopped. He would sit in his chair with a four-pack of Guinness – his favourite – and you could not speak to him while the match was on. For him and so many others, cricket was not just a game; it was a source of pride. In the 70s and 80s, the West Indies team, led by legends like Clive Lloyd, dominated the sport. Watching them win was not just about sport – it was about seeing Black excellence on a global stage.

It was not just Black Caribbeans who loved cricket either. The Indian community in Manchester felt the same pride. At places like Lancashire Cricket Club in Old Trafford, you would see a mix of cultures, all cheering together. It felt like home away from home, a reminder of where we came from and how far we could go.

Looking back, music and cricket were not just hobbies – they were anchors, holding us steady in a world that often did not see or hear us. Whether it was the soul beats at Wigan Casino or the reggae rhythms in Moss Side, these were the spaces where we could truly be ourselves.

The mills in Lancashire, like the one where I worked, played a significant role in the cotton industry. This industry was intricately connected to the transatlantic slave trade. Enslaved Africans, including my ancestors, were forced to labour on cotton plantations, producing the raw materials which fuelled these mills. This historical context added a heavy layer of meaning to my work in the mill for a mail order catalogue company; I was continuing a legacy of exploitation and resilience.

William Blake's phrase 'dark Satanic mills' from his poem 'And did those feet in ancient time' resonated deeply with me. Blake criticised the Industrial Revolution's impact on England, and his words took on a profound significance knowing that the cotton passing through my hands had a history soaked in the blood and sweat of enslaved people. The mills, while a testament to industrial progress, were also a stark reminder of the dehumanisation and suffering endured by those who went before me.

Working in the mill, I faced my own set of challenges. The echoes of historical injustices were ever-present, influencing how I was perceived and treated but, despite these challenges, my strong bonds with a diverse group of girls like me was ever-present and formed an informal network of camaraderie, psychological safety, and laughter.

My story, like many others, reflects the intertwined histories of industrialisation and human exploitation. Little did I know that these experiences and insights would become the catalyst for my twenty-five-year career in social justice policy. Over the years, I developed strategic networks and dedicated myself to serving those on the margins of society and the victims of systemic racism.

It is a call to remember and honour the sacrifices of those who came before us, and to strive for a future where all contributions are recognised and valued. There, amid the humdrum of machinery and the rhythm of production lines and twelve-hour shifts, I found a sense of belonging and sisterhood that crossed racial religious barriers. This reflected a time in Lancashire's history of multiculturalism. My friends were — Hindu, Muslim, African, Irish — all coming together in a symphony of shared experiences and mutual respect with a commonality that we were all working class young women.

Daily work at this period of my life became a testament to unity and camaraderie. We walked to work together and clocked in, exchanging stories on the way to work and laughter along the way. We would dine together and, at home time, we would clock out.

In this vibrant tapestry of close friendships, I never felt the need to wear a Superwoman cape. There, in the embrace of diverse Lancashire, I felt seen, heard, and valued for who I was. Our differences were not barriers but bridges that connected us, enriching our lives with shared experiences and mutual understanding. In loose terms, it was what I would come to experience and recognise as belonging to an informal women of colour network. My community of close friendships was truly diverse and consisted of Saheera, a Muslim, Prabha and Pushpa who were both Hindi and my dear friend Cath, who was an Asian Ugandan. We would walk to work together, take our lunch break together, work paid overtime together, wait for each other to catch the bus, or walk home together and share our confidence. There was no need to ask, do not tell anyone we never did, we were so close. I was later to attend weddings of these friends and their subsequent children's weddings. What a privilege to grow up among a group of global, diverse women of difference race or religion. None of these issues, which concern many today, ever cropped up between us. It wasn't an issue — there were too many commonalities. We were all second-generation British, our parents invited here by the government to support and help build back Britain after World War II. Our commonalities were our strength. We were all working-class women of colour who lived in the same area of Lancashire and worked in a factory.

While this group of young women did not consciously create a network, as I reflect on this period of my life, this is what I now know to be a women's community network or the beginnings of one, shared values, peer support.

"Suck Salt Through a Wooden Spoon" (Jamaican saying)

Education The University Years

University seemed like a distant dream reserved for those born into a different social class. For a long time, I believed the life I was heading toward would be determined by the need to work straight out of school and contribute to support the household. There was one working wage in the household, and I needed to do my bit. My working-class roots grounded me in values such as hard work, respect, community. Yet, deep down, I had a burning desire to continue learning. I was tired of well-meaning white friends and colleagues jumping uninvited into Black spaces to articulate matters relating to my lived experience, playing 'The White Saviour'. I was just as capable as everyone else of achieving my ambitions far beyond the council estate where I had lived, and the Open University was the starting point which began a trajectory which changed my life. It provided a way to access education without stepping away from my obligations and responsibilities. The Open University was built on the concept that learning should be open and accessible to everyone, regardless of background and constraints. This was something that resonated deeply with my own values: access for all and the ability to better oneself no matter what the obstacles.

I began my academic journey with the Open University, juggling a full-time job, and a Saturday/Sunday in the commercial world which helped to pay my university fees and all the domestic responsibilities which came with owning one's own home as a solo first-time buyer and homeowner. The requirements of the Open University at that time were to undertake a monthly assignment, watch BBC2 OU programme where appropriate, according to which academic study one was undertaking, and attend a local monthly group class tutorial. Each module required intense focus, and each year ended with an exam I had to prepare for while balancing the rest of my life.

I quickly learned that organisation was key. There was no room for procrastination. Taping radio programmes on BBC2, rewinding cassette tapes and late-night lectures, I committed myself to my studies. The assignments were rigorous, and I had to reach at least 40 per cent to pass each assignment marked by a tutor — or retake it. It may not seem like much, but each score felt hard-earned and significant, and fortunately I achieved higher than a 40 per cent pass mark for my assignments. I could not afford the time to do a retake of an assignment and so was very focused on the tasks. Every exam that I completed validated that I was capable and that I was good enough, navigating a society where the odds were stacked against me. I recall my wise mother would often say to me that there will be times where I must "suck salt through a wooden spoon". Imagining the act of this made my toes curl. It is a metaphorical phrase often used by my elders to describe enduring challenging times or overcoming struggles.

This phrase encapsulated the resilience and fortitude required to survive when resources were scarce, opportunities were limited, and the very systems meant to support were rigged against us. The reality was harsh: socio-economically, people like me were written off before we even had a chance to prove ourselves, growing up under the shadow of pre-1976 biases before the Race Relations Act made its promises. The hidden barriers and insidious biases seemed insurmountable. Yet, I persisted, refusing to let the world's expectations dictate my worth. Each challenge was a grain of salt, each triumph a testament to my resilience. My journey was not just about surviving, but about thriving despite the unspoken limitations placed upon me, proving that even when you are asked to suck salt through a wooden spoon, you can still turn your trials into triumphs.

Over the course of seven consecutive years, I chipped away at my first degree. For me this was more than just a piece of paper — it was the key to a door that had always seemed distant and shut. As part of my studies, I spent time at summer schools across the country, diving deeper into subjects which not only fascinated me but nourished me. I spent time at Durham University studying psychology, Bath University opened my eyes to social policy, and Liverpool and Manchester University gave me the chance to explore diversity, welfare and American policy and studies. These experiences opened a whole new world, one that I never thought I would be part of. Suddenly, I was surrounded by academics, engaging in conversations I had only imagined. I stayed in halls, collaborating with peers, and made lifelong friends who came from a variety of diverse backgrounds and classes, proving that education was not just for the elite.

A pivotal moment came in 1997 when I was introduced to the work by Professor Stuart Hall at the Open University headquarters in Milton Keynes. Until that moment, I had no idea who Professor Stuart Hall was, nor the immense impact he had in the field of sociology. I sat there in the lecture theatre mesmerised, as he spoke about race, identity power and privilege representation and reality with a depth and clarity that left me in awe. His work made me rethink how I viewed the world, and how I viewed myself even. I had never seen anyone weave together academic brilliance on matters of race with such an acute awareness of the social realities I had lived. Suddenly, sociology was not just an abstract concept — it was the prism through which my own experiences could be understood. Hall's work gave voice to the complexities of identity and class, and I found myself deeply moved. His ideas resonated with my own life.

It was also through the Open University that I encountered the work of the poet Benjamin Zephaniah, though in an unexpected way. I listened to an OU tape for the course that was known as D103, part of my social sciences module, when his voice came through the speakers. His raw, rhythmic poetry, along with his wonderful Birmingham accent, was unlike anything that I had ever experienced. Thank goodness I kept all my tapes! It was captivating and unapologetically honest, speaking to experiences of inequality, race, culture, and injustice. I was required to write an assignment based on this tape, and it pushed me to think deeply about the intersections of race, class, social structures and oppression. They were subjects that at the time were never mainstream, front and centre. His poetry was just something I had to analyse for the course; it was a challenge to think more critically about the world that I lived in.

Strangely, as I was discovering these remarkable thinkers, I was still struggling with this imposter syndrome-like feeling. No matter how well I did, a part of me could not shake off the feeling that I did not truly belong in these academic circles. I had not passed my eleven-plus, the exam that had dictated the academic future of so many in my generation. That failure had stuck with me, festering quietly in the background. But each time I passed another exam at Manchester University, where the Open University held its annual tests, I felt that barrier crumble just a little bit more. The Open University was showing me that the traditional route was not the only path to success.

Despite the doubts, I kept going, passing every annual exam, and meeting every submission deadline. Each small victory reinforced a self-worth and a validation to the world, proving that regardless of where I started, I had earned my place in society. The Open University was not just an institution; it was a lifeline, a bridge between where I wanted to go and how I was going to get there. It allowed me to work, to live my life, and still pursue the education I aspired to. More importantly, it validated my belief that everyone — no matter their background and race or gender — deserves a chance to succeed in life, which is the reason why I am such an advocate for the Open University and, after all these years, I can still recall my personal identifier number!

By the time I graduated at Bridgewater Hall, Manchester, in 2004, I had grown, not just academically but personally as I learned to navigate the world that had once seemed closed to me. I was able think critically on things that mattered to me, such as social justice. The Open University opened the door, but it was me who walked through that door, proving to myself that I was capable, worthy, and — despite my lingering doubts — I was not an imposter at all. But I still wore the Superwoman cape — I was getting too comfortable wearing the cape that shielded me from facing past traumas and fears.

Reflecting on my journey over the past seven years, I am filled with an immense sense of accomplishment and self-discovery. Pursuing an Open University degree while managing the demands of full-time work, holding down a Saturday job, and being a first-time homeowner has taught me invaluable lessons about resilience, time management, and perseverance. Each year brought new challenges, from annual exams to monthly academic tutorials and summer schools, all of which required meticulous planning and unwavering determination.

This period of my life was under my Superwoman cape and pre-menopause, which meant that I had an elevated level of oestrogen, thus an elevated level of energy and greater focus. Balancing work and studies, I mastered the art of prioritising tasks and maintaining a disciplined schedule. Being solely responsible for managing my mortgage and household further honed my organisational skills, teaching me the importance of self-reliance and adaptability. Navigating the daily balancing of systemic discrimination prevalent through policies and systems, particularly during my career period when I was employed within the police service, added another layer of complexity.

Throughout these challenges, my mother's words still rang in my ears about having to work twice as hard just to be "good enough" as my fellow white friends, even when we came from the same socio-economic background. This statement drove me to push myself continually, striving to exceed expectations in all areas of my life.

This intense learning and hard work have shown me the depths of my capabilities, reinforcing my belief in the power of dedication and tenacity. It has also underscored the significance of self-care, as finding moments to recharge was crucial amid the chaos.

Achieving my degree has not only expanded my knowledge but also profoundly shaped my identity, proving that with the right mindset and support, I can overcome any obstacle. My journey is a testament to the strength and resilience that lie within us, encouraging others to pursue their dreams no matter the hurdles they may face.

Practical Tools for Navigating Corporate Spaces

Building on these insights, this book will not only explore the research findings but also provide actionable strategies to enhance individual and organisational approaches to diversity and inclusion.

1. Enhancing Psychological Safety:
- **Develop Authenticity Workshops**: Organisations can implement workshops that encourage open dialogue and authenticity in the workplace, helping Black women feel more psychologically safe.

- **Mentorship Programmes**: Setting up formal mentorship programmes that pair Black women with senior leaders can provide the support needed to navigate corporate challenges.

2. Prioritising Health and Wellness:
- **Boundary-Setting Techniques**: Encourage employees to set clear boundaries around work hours and responsibilities, reducing burnout and promoting work–life balance.

- **Wellness Resources**: Companies should offer tailored wellness programmes that acknowledge the unique stressors Black women face, incorporating mental health support, meditation sessions, and wellness days.

3. Building Resilience:
- **Peer Support Groups**: Setting up peer support groups within organisations can foster a sense of belonging and shared resilience.

- **Leadership Development**: Provide access to leadership training specifically designed for women of colour, helping to build confidence and skills for navigating corporate hierarchies.

4. Fostering Leadership and Representation:
- **Diversity in Leadership**: Companies should focus on diversity in their recruitment processes, with specific targets for promoting Black women to leadership positions.
- **Role Models and Allies**: Highlighting Black women in leadership through internal communications and events can create a more inclusive and inspiring corporate culture.

Conclusion

This data offers valuable insights that challenge traditional corporate narratives and highlight the resilience and adaptability of Black women in these spaces. This book is a call to action for organisations to not only recognise these challenges but also implement meaningful strategies that promote inclusion, psychological safety, and well-being.

In the chapters that follow, we will delve deeper into these themes, offering both research-backed insights and practical tools designed to empower Black women navigating the complexities of the corporate world. This is more than just a book; it is a resource, a guide, and a testament to the strength and resilience of Black women who continue to thrive despite the odds.

The Hidden Impact of EDI Research: Bridging Communities and Building Accountability"

As a leader, working with a busy local provider, part of the NHS system, with a remit to review, advise and make cultural change, had unique challenges. For one there was the hierarchical nature of the NHS made for gatekeeping and informal networks not open to myself, yet I was required to understand the nuances which come with leading on matters relating EDI working in the community and internally and within a busy HR department.

During my academic studies at the University of Bradford, I chose to focus my research on the experiences of the transgender community in accessing primary and secondary care. This work, born from an invitation to a Yorkshire-based transgender community group, involved developing structured questions and creating a safe space for fourteen individuals – those who had transitioned from male to female and female to male – to share their first-hand experiences. A significant finding was the absence of Black transgender members within the group, which revealed a hidden community within a hidden community and highlighted the depth of systemic inequities.

However, undertaking this project was not without its challenges. While the outcomes – guidance for lead nurses, matrons, and estate porters – were approved by the then Director of Nursing and the Trust Board, not everyone supported my decision to make these strategic cultural changes. Resistance to EDI work is common. Many individuals questioned its necessity, adopting an attitude of "as long as I can access services, what does it really matter?" Yet, I passionately believe there is both a moral imperative and a legal requirement to ensure equitable access and experiences for all humanity. This belief guided me through moments of opposition, requiring strong project management and leadership to remain focused on the vision, manage those difficult conversations and listen to differing opinions.

I am aware, dear reader, that my reflections may differ from your own. As someone with family members who have personally experienced unequal access to health resources, I feel the weight of this work profoundly. For me, this research was more than academic — it was about ensuring that marginalised voices are heard and acted upon in meaningful ways. Strategic change, particularly within EDI, requires resilience and a commitment to the long-term goal of justice, even when immediate support is lacking. This journey affirmed my conviction that leadership in EDI is not just about policies; it is about addressing inequalities head-on and doing right by all members of our shared humanity.

Leadership Life Lessons
Seven key leadership life lessons I took away.

1. **Embrace Authenticity**: Stay true to your values and beliefs, even when faced with opposition. Authentic leadership fosters trust and respect.

2. **Resilience in Adversity**: Develop the ability to bounce back from setbacks and keep pushing forward. Adversity can be a powerful teacher.

3. **Strategic Vision**: Always keep the bigger picture in mind. Having a clear vision helps you stay focused on your goals, even when facing challenges.

4. **Champion Collaboration**: Building bridges and collaborating with diverse communities can create a stronger,

more inclusive environment. Embrace collaboration as a source of strength.

5. **Self-Care and Boundaries**: Recognise the importance of self-care. Setting boundaries is crucial to maintain your well-being and effectiveness as a leader.

6. **Continuous Learning**: Always be open to learning and growing. Embrace new perspectives and skills, which can enhance your leadership journey.

7. **Empower Others**: Lift others as you rise. Encourage and support those around you, creating a ripple effect of positive change.

Leading in a men's prison in the UK requires a unique set of skills and competences which require a combination of not only understanding diversity, equality and inclusion and an ability to work effectively in a challenging environment of cultural competence. It also requires the ability to understand and appreciate people from diverse backgrounds, including race, religion and all the UK-recognised protected characteristics for men within the Equality Act 2010 and the Human Rights Act 1998, and how they apply within the prison system as I write this book. Legislation awareness and a key, in-depth knowledge of law was key in this role, as I had to respond to enquiries on behalf of the Senior prison Governor of the prison at that time of my employment. from solicitors on matters around human rights violations. Understanding the prison population and an awareness of the needs through the lens of diversity was key. While the prison population was diverse, there was still an over representation of Black and brown prisoners per prison population, which during my time was approximately 30 per cent resident in this prison. There was also a high rate of foreign nationals incarcerated during this time. A Foreign National Prisoner (FNP) is an individual who is not a British citizen and who has been convicted of a criminal offence and is serving a custodial sentence in a prison in England and Wales, or across the UK. This includes people who may have lived in the UK for many years but do not hold British nationality, as well as those who have recently entered the country.

Foreign National prisoners are subject to the same criminal justice processes as UK nationals; however, they may also be subject to additional immigration proceedings, including the possibility of deportation either during or at the end of their sentence under the UK Borders Act 2007 or the Immigration Act 1971.

This group is highly diverse, encompassing a wide range of nationalities, cultural backgrounds, and legal statuses. Many face unique challenges in custody, such as language barriers, cultural isolation, limited family contact, and uncertainty about their future—particularly if they are at risk of removal or deportation. These additional layers can significantly impact their mental health, access to rehabilitation, and fair treatment within the system.

Communication and people skills, empathy, and the ability to gain trust and rapport were key, enabling me to hear the diverse perspectives of prisoners who wanted to not only be heard but understood. And on many occasions, I would receive letters from prisoners asking that I see them to hear their issues. Training and advocacy skills were needed in this role, as I had to design and deliver training for my team and for prisoners advocating for marginalised groups within the prison system.

Analysis and problem-solving skills were key in this role, as my priority was to address the issues of race and ensure that the recommendations from the Zahid Mubarek report was adhered to and that the prison was ready for HMIP (Her Majesty's Inspectorate of Prisons). I needed an ability to analyse demographic data to recognise trends and areas where diversity and inclusion efforts need to be improved. Strategic thinking was a key requirement as I developed and implemented diversity strategies that aligned to prison policies and their goals. Leadership and influence skills were necessary as my work involved collaborating with stakeholders such as primary care colleagues and external partners, and government agencies to promote diversity, equality and inclusion.

The ability to lead and manage change while maintaining composure in high-pressure and often stressful environments was essential. Equally critical was the capacity to remain flexible, adjusting strategies in real time as circumstances evolved. A core competence in this context was the commitment to confidentiality—safeguarding sensitive personal information, particularly in relation to prisoners' diverse backgrounds. This required a nuanced understanding of privacy, respect, and cultural sensitivity, ensuring that diversity-related issues were handled with discretion and integrity.

Being a principled leader was key in that my leadership decisions were ethical, also ensuring that the decisions I made were aligned with legal frameworks and fair standards of the prison service, promoting social justice for all. The ability to balance security considerations with ensuring that diversity and inclusion was key, as the environment required safety.

The cultural environment within a prison was often volatile, so a high level of emotional intelligence and the ability to understand different emotional states, backgrounds and behaviours and how to approach sensitive issues within a prison context was key. My career working within the police environment and with a diverse range of community stakeholders ensured that I was able to develop a high degree of emotional intelligence along with crises management skills, which I developed within the police service. I was on duty when the IRA bomb attack in Manchester city centre occurred and myself and another senior manager were responsible for the management of sixteen police traffic wardens which reported into the Greater Manchester Police traffic inspector. At the time it was Inspector Swan at Bootle Street police station.

As an adult, those early lessons in self-abandonment resurfaced vigorously. Managing and leading within a category-B men's prison prison's senior leadership team, I found myself again pushing my needs aside, focusing solely on the demands of the job and the expectations of others. But, this time, the stakes were higher, the consequences of neglecting my own well-being were more severe. The question began to haunt me: can I be my own liberation?

I realised that liberation starts with the acknowledgement of one's own worth. It requires unearthing the feelings long buried, recognising the traumas endured, and confronting the fears which have taken root. For years I had navigated life with my heart carefully tucked away — a protection mechanism that had served its purposes but now threatened my well-being. To be free, I had to reclaim those parts of myself I had abandoned.

The journey toward self-liberation is not an easy one. It demands courage, the willingness to face uncomfortable truths, and the strength to prioritise oneself. It requires redefining boundaries, asserting one's own needs, and allowing joy and laughter back into the fold.

The strong Black woman schema can often be described as a pillar of strength, self-sufficiency and resilience of someone who is multi-dimensional and able to function as a shield and ably adapt to cultural situations and display caretaking qualities.

However, the impact of institutional racism on the Black women can have a significant impact, which certainly caused me to stay under the protected wing of my Superwoman cape. I have highlighted three key areas which affect Black women.

Case Study: "Chantel, NHS Deputy Director"
Chantel was one of only two Black women at her level in a large NHS trust. On paper, she had everything: a six-figure salary, influence in national healthcare policy, and the respect of her peers. But privately, Chantel lived in constant anxiety that she was "on borrowed time".

Despite her achievements, she avoided taking holidays, declined offers to speak at leadership conferences, and rarely treated herself to anything that wasn't on sale. She once said, "If I relax, I might drop the ball. If I shine too brightly, someone might dim my light."

When she bought her first home, she filled it with clearance items and second-hand furnishings — beautiful to others, but chosen more out of fear than joy. Her mindset wasn't one of celebration — it was of survival. And underneath it all was a gnawing belief: *I have to keep proving I deserve to be here.*

Eventually, after a health scare and coaching support, Chantel began to see the emotional cost of wearing the Superwoman cape. She started unlearning the poverty mindset that told her she had to shrink to stay safe. She stepped into her leadership not from fear, but from worth.

Breaking Free from the Poverty Mindset

I grew up believing that working twice as hard was the only way to survive. Financial security, I was taught, came from relentless effort — never saying no and always proving my worth. Even when I stepped into leadership roles, the shadow of scarcity followed me. It whispered that at any moment, everything could be taken away, that I didn't truly belong, that I had to overperform just to stay afloat.

This is the poverty mindset: the deep-rooted fear that no matter how much you achieve, it's never enough, that you're one mistake away from losing everything. Born from generations forced to fight for a seat at the table, it begins as a tool for survival. But in leadership, it becomes a burden, feeding imposter syndrome and locking us into the Superwoman role, where exhaustion is mistaken for excellence.

Despite my qualifications and hard-won experience, I often felt like an outsider in boardrooms and senior leadership meetings — like I had snuck in and was waiting to be exposed. So I pushed harder. I said yes when I wanted to say no. I sacrificed my well-being and wore burnout like a badge of honour.

I see now how the poverty mindset travelled with me — quietly, persistently. It wasn't just in the early days of my career; it stayed with me even when I had 'arrived'. I remember buying my dream home — a milestone I should've celebrated. Instead, I immediately calculated, over-budgeted, and prepared for the worst. When furnishing my space, I gravitated toward the cheapest options — not because I lacked resources, but because I was still operating from fear.

That's the trap of the poverty mindset: it convinces you that safety lies in shrinking, not shining. It shows up as over-responsibility, hypervigilance, and a fear of resting or delegating. You wear the

Superwoman cape not out of pride, but as armour. It is heavy, burdensome, and ultimately unsustainable.

It took time — and intention — to realise that my choices, even in abundance, were still shaped by fear. That's imposter syndrome. That's fear dressed as humility.

But true leadership isn't born from lack. It's born from alignment. And abundance isn't just about finances — it's emotional, spiritual, and internal. I had to unlearn survival mode, to reprogram my compass from "just in case" to "just because I deserve it".

True leadership doesn't stem from lack — it grows from alignment.

" It wasn't enough to write about abundance — I had to live it and, most importantly, believe I was worthy of it.

Leadership Life Lessons: From Scarcity to Sovereignty

1. **Recognise How Fear Manifests in Leadership**
   Are you overworking, under-investing in yourself, or afraid to rest? These may signal a scarcity mindset — even in senior roles.

2. **Release the Superwoman cape**
   Burnout is not a badge of honour. Leadership draws its power from presence, not perfection. Say no. Delegate. Honour your energy and capacity.

3. **Lead from the Present, Not the "What If"**
   Celebrate your wins. Choose joy over fear. Your leadership journey deserves rest, beauty, and abundance — not just because you've earned it, but because you are enough.

The Impact of Institutional Racism on Black women:

- **Barrier to Advancement**: Black women often meet a 'concrete ceiling' in their career progression, a metaphor for the almost impenetrable barriers preventing them from advancing into leadership roles. Despite qualifications and experience, they are often overlooked for promotions or strategic projects, often due to biases about their capabilities and leadership styles.

- **Code-Switching and Self-Censorship**: To fit into white spaces, Black women may feel pressured to suppress aspects of their cultural identity, language, and expressions. This 'code-switching' can be exhausting and hinder authentic self-expression, thereby affecting job satisfaction and engagement.

- **Lack of Mentorship and Sponsorship**: Institutional racism also manifests in the lack of mentorship and sponsorship opportunities for Black women, leaving them without the networks.

Liberation – Leadership in a Police Force Bridging Cultural Divides and Building Trust

I was employed between 1990 and 2004 at Greater Manchester Police force, one of the largest police forces in England. At the time this force employed approximately 10,000 police officers and staff which included approximately 3,000 police staff. Despite serving one of the most diverse urban populations in the country, the demographic makeup of the force—particularly within its senior ranks—did not reflect the communities it was meant to protect. According to the 2001 Census, Greater Manchester had a population approaching 2.5 million, with an increasingly multicultural and multi-ethnic profile. Yet, the force's internal culture and composition lagged behind these societal shifts, contributing to growing discontent, mistrust, and a palpable sense of exclusion both within the organisation and among the wider public.

During my career within the police service as a member of police staff, there was only one Black police officer that achieved the rank of Chief Constable across the entire British police force. Michael Fuller held this historic position at Kent Constabulary from 2004 to 2010, marking a significant yet isolated moment of representation at the highest level of policing leadership.

Black women in Leadership

The British Police Service
In 1990 I was appointed into Greater Manchester Police (GMP) as a member of police staff. This was at a time when GMP and all other forces had recruitment requirements reflecting standards common in the wider UK police forces at the time. These requirements often included criteria that inadvertently limited the diversity of its workforce, particularly for women, individuals from ethnic minority backgrounds, and those with disabilities. Standing at five feet, my height may have precluded me from the police staff application process. To help set some context, here is a short outline of the then recruitment criteria:

1. Height Requirements for Women
- **Height Standard**: During the early 1990s, GMP, like other UK police forces, had a minimum height requirement for recruits. For women, this was typically around **five feet four inches (162 cm)**, while for men, it was around **five feet eight inches (172 cm)**.

- **Impact**: These height requirements disproportionately excluded women and certain ethnic groups where average height statistics fell below these thresholds.

2. Eligibility for Individuals with Disabilities
- **Disabilities and Recruitment**: During this period, individuals with disabilities faced significant barriers to joining the police force. The predominant view was that physical fitness and unimpaired physical capability were essential for policing.

- **Reasoning**: The concept of 'operational readiness' often led to the exclusion of individuals with disabilities, even if their impairments would not have affected their ability to fulfil non-physical roles.

- **Legal Framework**: The Disability Discrimination Act was not introduced until 1995 and, prior to this, there were no legal requirements to accommodate or consider disabled candidates fairly.

3. Why and When Recruitment Requirements Were Overhauled
- **Height Requirement Abolishment**:
    - In the 1990s, forces began removing height requirements due to growing recognition that they were discriminatory.
    - By the late 1990s, GMP and other forces dropped this standard to comply with broader diversity goals.

Societal Impact of Recruitment Changes

1. Diversity, Equality, and Inclusion
- **Impact on Recruitment Practices:**
    - The removal of height requirements and the introduction of inclusive hiring policies allowed for a broader and more diverse pool of applicants. This began to challenge the traditional image of the police force as predominantly white, male, and able-bodied.
    - The implementation of competency-based assessments emphasised skills and potential rather than physical attributes, creating opportunities for women, ethnic minorities, and disabled individuals.

- **Community Representation:**
    - By reflecting the communities they served, police forces like GMP improved their ability to engage with diverse populations and address community-specific concerns, fostering trust and better communication.

2. Social Justice and Racial Tensions
- **Macpherson Report Recommendations:**
    - The fallout from the Macpherson Report following the Stephen Lawrence case highlighted systemic racism within UK policing and spurred critical reforms. Recruitment practices were identified as a key area for change, emphasising the importance of representation in building public confidence.

- **Community Relations**:
    - Police diversity efforts began to address long-standing mistrust between minority communities and law enforcement. Greater representation provided pathways for more culturally informed policing and equitable treatment.

3. Representation in Leadership
- **Michael Fuller's Appointment**:
    - Michael Fuller's tenure as Chief Constable of Kent Police from 2004 to 2010 marked a significant milestone as the UK's first (and, during that period, only) Black Chief Constable. His leadership symbolised progress but also highlighted the slow pace of change at police command senior levels.

- **Broader Implications**:
    - His appointment underscored the need for systemic change to address the barriers that limited diversity in leadership. It serves as a critical point of reflection on the progress still needed to achieve genuine equality.

The societal and systemic challenges addressed during this period resonate deeply with the themes of this book. The Superwoman expectations and the struggle for representation and equality within institutions mirrors the personal burden borne by women of colour to excel and represent their communities in spaces where they are underrepresented.

Eventually, I had to choose myself. I had to stop proving and start owning my space — without apology, without over-explanation, and without the weight of silence.

This part of my journey is essential to understanding why burning the Superwoman cape is about more than shedding perfectionism; it's about reclaiming joy, prioritising well-being, and leading from a place of wholeness rather than survival.

Strategic Staff Networks Operating Within the System: Black and Asian Police Association (BAPA)

have been a member of proactive inclusive and proactive networks and been a member of networks which have only two or three members operating, while other members eat from the fruits of the labour of others with no real impact, leading to those few active members burning themselves out.

expresses the idea that the oppressive systems ("the master's house") cannot be dismantled using the same methods or structures ("the m

Burning My Superwoman Cape: Leadership Life Lessons for Black women Overcoming Imposter Syndrome

As Black women in leadership, we often feel the pressure to work twice as hard, prove our worth, and carry the weight of others' expectations. Imposter syndrome can whisper that we're not enough, while the Superwoman cape urges us to take on everything — without complaint, without rest. But I've learned that true leadership isn't about overworking or proving ourselves to others — it's about owning our power, setting boundaries, and thriving on our own terms.

Here are five leadership life lessons I have embraced to help silence imposter syndrome and finally let go of the Superwoman cape:

Keep a Record of Your Wins – You've Earned Them
Imposter syndrome thrives when we forget our own brilliance. Instead of doubting yourself, document your contributions – big and small. Write down the projects you've led, the challenges you've overcome, and the impact you've made. This isn't bragging; it's proof of your leadership. When self-doubt creeps in, or when it's time for promotions and performance reviews, let your own receipts remind you: you are more than qualified.

You Don't Have to Do It Alone – Build Your Personal Board of Advisors
Superwoman tries to do everything solo. But real leadership means knowing when to lean on others. Create a support system of mentors, sponsors, and trusted colleagues – people who will challenge and champion you. This board of advisors can help you navigate workplace challenges, deal with microaggressions, and remind you of your value when imposter syndrome makes you question it.

Expand Your Circle – Diverse Allies Can Open Doors
As Black women, we often find strength in community, but breaking free from imposter syndrome also means expanding our network beyond familiar spaces. Seek out allies from different backgrounds who can offer new perspectives, vouch for you in rooms you're not in yet, and help amplify your voice. The more visible and connected you are, the harder it is for imposter syndrome to convince you that you don't belong.

Be Strategic About Your Influence – You Deserve to be Heard
Being part of a Black staff network is more than just belonging – it's an opportunity to lead. But leadership isn't about doing the work; it's about making sure your ideas and efforts are recognised. Imposter syndrome may tell you to stay quiet, but instead, step forward. Learn

how to present your ideas with confidence. Use data, real-life success stories, and collaborations to strengthen your case. Build coalitions with other employee resource groups to create change that lasts.

Rest is Resistance – Prioritise Your Well-Being and Set Boundaries

Imposter syndrome often pushes us to overcompensate, saying yes to everything out of fear of being 'found out' or 'not doing enough' But constantly proving ourselves leads to burnout. It's time to let go of that mindset. Set boundaries around your time and energy. Say no to unpaid DEI work that isn't valued. Prioritise self-care, whether that's therapy, rest, or time with your sister circle. Find joy outside of work. You are enough – without overworking, without overgiving, without the Superwoman.

These lessons are personal to me because I've lived them. I know what it's like to feel like I must do it all, to second-guess my place at the table, and to push myself past exhaustion just to prove I belong. But I also know that imposter syndrome is a liar, and the Superwoman cape is too heavy to carry forever.

Sister, it's time to burn the cape. You don't have to prove your worth – you already have it. Now, lead from a place of confidence, community, and self-care. You belong.

Find and Leverage Mentors and Allies

Seek out mentors and allies who are not only within the network but also hold influential positions outside it. Look for individuals who can offer career guidance, open doors to opportunities, and advocate on your behalf. Establish regular check-ins to discuss your career goals, seek advice on navigating corporate politics, and get insights into unwritten rules that may affect your progress. If possible, engage with a coach who can help strategise your career path and build resilience against workplace challenges.

Initiate a Reverse Mentorship relationship with a senior leader to bring new perspectives to their understanding of diversity and your experiences as a Black woman in the company.

Set Clear Objectives for Your Involvement

Before joining the network, define what you want to achieve. Are you looking to build a support system, develop leadership skills, influence company policies, or gain visibility? Setting clear aims will help you stay focused and make the most of your participation. Use the network as a platform to highlight and share your skills and insights and take on leadership roles in strategic projects or operational committees which align with your career aspirations and align with the networks values and aims. Over the years I have found not only inner strength and resilience through membership of these networks but also been able to share my own insights and been seen and heard while we nourish others.

Community tensions were extremely high during this period, fuelled by rising gun crime and a deep mistrust between the police and local communities. Religious tensions also ran high, particularly during key periods of religious observance. The tragic murder of Black teenager Stephen Lawrence in 1993, and the subsequent publication of the Macpherson Report in 1999, became pivotal moments in British policing. The report's findings, which identified institutional racism within the police service, marked a watershed and catalysed urgent calls for change.

It was against this backdrop of unrest that the BAPA, as it was first known, was formed.

I was appointed as the first BAPA coordinator of the association. My role was complex and critical and involved a matrix strategic leadership and management approach across different systems which helped to facilitate collaboration and resource sharing across different departments, community groups and networks to address the regional complex social justice and internal workforce issues effectively. The coordinators' role was integral to the success of the BAPA, ensuring that it remained active, influential, and aligned with its members' needs and the broader strategic objectives of the police force and national recommendations from the Macpherson Report.

Aims and Objectives of BAPA During My Period of Tenure:

- Improve workforce representation through recruitment, retention, and progression initiatives of Black and Asian staff.

- Review and improve current policies, systems and institutional practices which unwittingly discriminate and disadvantage Black and Asian staff.

- Prevent and reduce crime, harm, and protect people.

As part of the BAPA, my coordination role involved:

- **Administration Support** – Providing direct support to the chair and deputy chair of the police staff network, organising meetings, preparing agendas, and taking minutes.

- Managing the network's communication channels, including emails, newsletters, and social media.

- Maintain records, including membership lists and meeting notes.

- **Event planning and coordination** — organising events, workshops, and seminars that promote race equality and inclusion within the police service.

- Coordinating cultural awareness programmes and initiatives to enable staff to be better educated on matters which affect the Black community of Greater Manchester.

- **Liaison and Advocacy** — Acting as the liaison between the network, police leadership and external stakeholders.

- Advocating for the interest of and concerns of Black staff within the *wider force*.

- Ensuring the network's views are represented in the force's policies and decision-making processes.

- **Supporting and Guidance** — "Providing advice and support to network members by signposting appropriate resources for wellbeing, career development, and addressing discrimination. Facilitating mentorship programmes that connect junior colleagues with more experienced professionals for guidance and development."

- **Strategic Planning**

Assisting in the development and implementation of the network's strategic goals and objectives. Monitoring the progress of diversity and inclusion initiatives within the police force and providing feedback to enable service improvements.

- **Community Engagement**

    Building relationships with community groups, particularly those which represented the Black and Asian communities across the region.

- Working with the Force Positive Action Group and coordination of outreach police career programmes.

- **Resource Management**

    Working with HR managing the network's budget and other resources effectively.

I recall the formal launch of the BAPA at Manchester Town Hall, an event sponsored by one of the assistant chief constables on behalf of GMP, which underscored the importance of our mission to promote and improve race equality within the police service. Under my coordination, BAPA achieved remarkable success, most notably in the significant increase in the recruitment of Black and Asian police officers. This was due to the targeted outreach initiatives within Manchester's rich and diverse communities which were instrumental in encouraging underrepresented groups to consider careers in policing.

Our efforts extended beyond the local context, as I had the honour of representing the force on a global stage at the US Black Police Force Leadership conference in Atlanta, Georgia. There I was tasked by my own force with a critical project to evaluate US police recruitment processes, which offered invaluable insights which I reported back to the BAPA and the police force.

This was not just a symbolic gesture; it directly contributed to making strategic improvements within our own recruitment practices. Our internal network was driven by pride and a collective's sense of purpose, and confidence that our work was making a real difference. The success of the BAPA was a powerful testament to the power of staff networks, collaboration and system working.

Driving Change: The Impact of the BAPA on Greater Manchester Police Recruitment Campaigns

- **Advocacy for Change**:
    - Through the Black Police Association, I was able to play a pivotal role in implementing Macpherson's recommendations. This included advising on recruitment strategies to attract candidates from underrepresented backgrounds and fostering community dialogue to rebuild trust.

- **Improving Community Confidence**:
    - Through working with other members of the Positive Action Team within HR Recruitment, I was delighted to have been able to contribute to the increased visibility of Black and Asian police officers from the Greater Manchester region, highlighting policing as a viable career for individuals from diverse backgrounds. These efforts supported a gradual shift in public perception, positioning GMP as a more inclusive institution.

Domestic Violence

Trigger Warning

I never thought it would happen to me. I had always heard the stories, seen the statistics, even dealt with domestic violence through my voluntary work. I could not understand why victims would lie and why they would cover up for their abusers. But as I write this as a survivor of domestic abuse, I now know how this can happen.

He had been out drinking with his friends, and when we came back to my home as we had agreed, he expected me to be waiting for him, submissive, ready. But when I was not, he became violent. He pinned me down on the bed, straggling me, and when I resisted, he punched me in the face. I can still see the blood splattering onto the bedroom walls, still feeling the sting of his fist. Sheer terror flooded me.

I called the police. I had only just been appointed as police staff into the force and, as the knock came on my door, I recognised both officers, a man and a woman. The shame was suffocating. How could I let them see me like this? He sat there crying. We were both separated. I sat at the top of my stairs speaking to the officers, and he was dealt with by the male officer. The shame of officers seeing me in this state was overwhelming. My then boyfriend, the man, was told to leave my house and go to his own house and, true of the stories I had heard from other abuse survivors, he called me when he got home crying and pleading with me, apologising for what he had done. It was the cruellest twist to hear him in tears after what he had done to me, and still, a part of me wanted to believe him.

I remember standing in A&E on a Sunday morning trying to explain away the bruising to my nose with a clumsy lie about falling downstairs. I now understood. The shame, the horror, the shock all consumed me. How could I, a strong Black woman, let this happen? I remember that I could hardly look the health professional in the eyes. The anxiety of him seeing through my words was crushing. It made me feel like a fraud in my own life, pretending to have everything together when inside I was broken. I recall seeing one of the officers weeks later and pulling him to one side seeking assurance that what he witnessed was not to be shared with anyone. I recall him responding to me and saying, "Do not worry, love. The number of calls that we receive to attend our own colleagues; you would be surprised. Your secret is safe with us."

There I was shaping policies to protect others, but who was protecting me? Throughout my career in these institutions, imposter syndrome was a constant companion. I was leading, advising, and driving strategic change, yet I often questioned whether I truly belonged in these high-stakes spaces. Was I there because of my skills and expertise, or was I simply a token – a box ticked for diversity? The tension between knowing my worth and constantly needing to prove it sat heavy on my shoulders.

And then, behind closed doors, another battle raged. The violence I worked to challenge in the world around me had found its way into my personal life. Domestic violence does not discriminate – it reaches women in boardrooms, in leadership positions, in spaces where they are expected to be strong. I was helping institutions address injustice yet privately enduring my own.

For so long, I had been conditioned to endure, to keep going, to lead despite the exhaustion, to wear the cape, even as it suffocated me. But as I navigated my personal reality, I came to a painful realisation: strength is not about how much you can endure – it is about knowing when to say, "No more."

This experience reinforced what I would later fully embrace in my leadership journey: burning the Superwoman cape is not only about work – it's about rejecting the expectation that we must carry burdens in silence.

For many Black women in leadership, the pressure to overperform, to overcompensate, and to be twice as good while suffering in silence is all too familiar. The imposter syndrome we feel is often not a result of lack, but of the deep-rooted messages that tell us we must prove our right to be in spaces we have already earned.

Ethnicity plays a role in the prevalence of domestic abuse. Individuals with a mixed ethnic background reported the highest rates at 7.9 per cent, while Asian individuals reported the lowest at 2 per cent. Specifically, mixed white and Black Caribbean women reported a notably high prevalence of 20.6 per cent.

My Liberation

The success I witnessed as the coordinator of the BAPA ignited a lifelong passion and belief for championing staff networks and community engagement. The tangible impact of our work, from significantly increasing the recruitment of Black and Asian police officers to representing the force globally, were more than just professional achievements – it was deeply personal. These experiences liberated me from the old ways of thinking that had been instilled in me during my upbringing, where negative programming and low expectations shaped my early life. Travelling to America and engaging with hundreds of Black and Asian police officers and staff opened my eyes to a world of possibilities I now believed were possible. The sense of empowerment and collective strength I felt during these interactions was profound, fuelling my commitment to ensuring that others would have support and encouragement to break free from beliefs. This journey marked a stark contrast to the narrow expectations set for me by my school and career advisors, who once suggested I pursue a career as a flower arranger – a recommendation that, while respectable, was grounded in limited perceptions of my potential.

The realisation that I could, and did, achieve career milestones far beyond what had been envisioned for me was both liberating and transformative, reinforcing my belief in the power of networks, mentorship, and community support in unlocking potential and overcoming barriers. These experiences have driven my continued dedication to fostering environments where diversity, equality and inclusion are celebrated and respected and where individuals are encouraged to dream and achieve self-actualisation more than they ever thought possible.

My work with BAPA was not just about changing the face of the police force because of the Macpherson Report; it was about working to change the narrative for myself and others, proving that with the right support, we can defy expectations and chart our own paths to success.

Exposure to these transformative experiences was not just the culmination of my journey within the police service but a crucial stepping stone to even greater personal and professional growth. The confidence I gained from successfully navigating and influencing complex systems within the police service empowered me to realise my own worth and potential beyond the traditional career paths laid out beyond me.

This newfound self-assurance eventually led to my departure from the police service, marking the beginning of a new chapter where I could fully embrace my unique strengths and aspirations. However, this path was not without its setbacks; it required immense resilience and unwavering confidence, and a sharp focus on my goals. A mantra which I often relied on was "stay in your lane", which became my guiding principle as I ventured into uncharted waters. By stepping away from conventional routes and forging my own, I made significant sacrifices, but these sacrifices have resulted in a life and career that truly reflect who I am and what I stand for. This journey has been a testament to the power of self-belief and the understanding that true success often lies outside of traditional boundaries.

Breaking Barriers: A Journey Beyond Expectations and Into Leadership

After fourteen years of dynamic and diverse leadership roles within the police service, I made the bold decision to take a career break and pursue full-time study for a Postgraduate Certificate in Education (PGCE) at Bolton University. This decision was not made lightly; it was born from a desire to break free from the potential of becoming institutionalised within the police system. Having served the community across Greater Manchester, represented the force regionally, and highlighted its efforts nationally and internationally, I realised the time had come to explore opportunities beyond the force. I yearned to broaden my horizons and gain new experiences, personally and professionally, outside the structure and routine of the police.

Leaving the service was daunting and exhilarating. I reflected deeply on what it meant to step away from a secure role — a position I had worked tirelessly to achieve — and into uncharted territory. It was not lost on me how far I had come from the young girl who had been written off after failing the eleven-plus exam. I had been told I would never amount to anything, yet there I was, making a courageous career decision that would propel me toward future strategic leadership roles. There was an undeniable pull toward experiencing the full immersion of academic study in a traditional university setting after spending seven years studying with the Open University. I missed the classroom environment — the intellectual exchange, the collaborative learning, and the camaraderie of peers.

The next twelve months became a transformative period. I relished the chance to teach, learn, and meet like-minded individuals who shared a passion for education. The opportunity to step outside my comfort zone into a new professional landscape was a challenge and a privilege. It reawakened my love for learning and reminded me that perseverance, ambition, and the courage to embrace change are crucial elements in personal and professional growth. This decision became a pivotal moment in my career, allowing me to gain the skills and confidence needed to take on even more significant and strategic roles in the future.

During my twelve-month career break to pursue the PGCE, I embraced the opportunity to collaborate with police trainers at the Bruche Police National Training Centre in Warrington. My role involved designing and delivering a comprehensive module on equality, diversity, and inclusion (EDI) for police probationers during their initial six weeks of training. Living on campus alongside fellow trainers allowed me to immerse myself fully in the training environment, facilitating both my university assessments and evaluations by the National Police Training School.

In 2003, the BBC broadcast *The Secret Policeman*, an undercover documentary that exposed instances of racism and bullying among recruits at Bruche. This revelation prompted national outrage and led to significant scrutiny of police training practices. Reflecting on my decision to engage with an institution later revealed to harbour such issues, I recognise a commitment to effecting change from within. Working in environments susceptible to volatility has profoundly shaped my professional identity, reinforcing the importance of confronting challenges directly and advocating for systemic improvements.

The aftermath of the documentary led to disciplinary action against several officers and trainers. Bruche Police Training Centre was closed in May 2006, with individual police forces assuming responsibility for training their recruits internally.

This experience imparted several leadership lessons that have been instrumental in my career development. I learned the value of fostering inclusive environments and the necessity of addressing prejudices proactively. Collaborating with diverse teams enhanced my ability to navigate complex interpersonal dynamics, assert authority appropriately, and respond effectively to spontaneous challenges. Additionally, designing training materials and assessment processes honed my skills in curriculum development and evaluative methodologies. These competencies have been pivotal in shaping my approach to leadership and management, emphasising the significance of inclusivity, adaptability, and continuous improvement.

Strategic Leadership Within a British Prison

Years later I found myself working as a senior manager in a category-B men's prison, a role fraught with challenges which evaluated every ounce of my resilience. In the wake of the national outcry following the murder of Zahid Mubarek at a young offender's institution — he was battered to death in his cell by a right-wing white inmate — a seismic shift in prison policies took place. The subsequent report and its recommendations led to my appointment as the diversity manager within the prison, a role that placed me at the forefront of investigating racist incidents and complaints by prisoners on behalf of the governor of the prison, and to undertake a strategic review of current institutional practices, policies, guidance and procedures. This addressed the diverse demographic of the prison population who had disabilities, those registered as foreign national prisoners and matters which may have related to the sexual orientation and safety of all within the sphere of ensuring that risk assessments addressed not only the security within the prison but the safety of prisoners.

During my employment within HMP service, the prison population in England and Wales showed consistent growth:

- In 2007, the average prison population was approximately 80,000, with a steady increase over the year due to tougher sentencing and policies like the use of longer custodial sentences.

- By 2008, this figure had risen to around 82,000.

- In 2009, the prison population further increased, reaching 83,000 to 84,000 by mid-year, depending on the specific monthly count.

These increases were influenced by changes in sentencing practices, such as the greater use of custodial sentences for violent and serious offences, as well as legislative reforms. Also, the introduction of measures like suspended sentence orders in 2005 led to breaches that also contributed to prison population growth. The role required annual reporting of diversity work into the Independent Monitoring Board and the prison SMT, and I would also report into the governor monthly, along with other SMT members.

The weight of my strategic responsibilities was immense, knowing that my efforts could potentially prevent another tragic loss of life. However, as part of my interview, I had to design a three-month strategy for how I would approach the task.

The intersection of race, representation, and my leadership role often highlighted the disparities within the system. As a Black woman in management, I met biases that mirrored the systemic inequities present in broader society. Yet, these challenges fuelled my commitment to creating spaces where the voices of marginalised groups — inmates and staff — were acknowledged and valued. This included developing programmes to raise cultural awareness among officers and implementing strategies to address the unique needs of prisoners from diverse backgrounds.

The work was demanding, yet it illuminated the resilience needed to lead in spaces where your very presence was an act of defiance against the norms. My role became a bridge — facilitating understanding, ensuring equality, and advocating for the systemic change necessary for a more humane and just prison environment.

My academic background in criminology and psychology became crucial tools which enabled me to critically analyse the culture and behaviours within the confines of a prison. I meticulously examined the systemic issues, the ingrained prejudices and the subtle yet pervasive practices that fostered a hostile environment for minority inmates. Through comprehensive investigations and persistent advocacy, I looked to create a prison culture that recognised and respected diversity, striving to dismantle the institutional and structural racism that had long been ignored. This role, while fraught with its own challenges and dangers, became a powerful avenue for enacting change, reaffirming my commitment to social justice and equality within the prison system.

The environment was harsh, the air thick with tension of confinement and desperation. Traumatic experiences were routine. Inmates, seeking to assert dominance or instil fear, would often tell me about the reasons for their sentences. I would never ask, one was never allowed to, but by segregation onto their own wing for their own protection from fellow prisoners, I knew who the sex offenders were.

Other prisoners would often come and tell me about the reasons for their sentences or share with me the sexual abuse they had personally experienced from childhood. Being the only senior Black woman manager in this prison, I oversaw the management of the race equality officer and the foreign national officer and disability officer. All three staff were operational prison officers. I often navigated the complex dynamics of an environment where senior managers, who were colloquially referred to as "suits", were met with a mix of respect and scepticism. I was in a suit!

I carried the added burden of feeling unsafe, the weight of my identity making me a target for intimidation from both sides of the cells. The threats were frequent, the intimidation relentless. Each day was a battle for psychological survival, where every interaction was laced with potential danger. The prison I walked daily to interact with prisoners and speak with them about their concerns, echoed the constant reminder of vulnerability. The wings, stained with years of despair and anger, seemed to close, whispering threats and reminders of the violence that lurked just beneath the surface. My role demanded authority and composure, yet inside, fear coiled tight, a constant, gnawing presence.

The life skills I developed in my youth – balancing multiple responsibilities, leading with both strength and empathy, and navigating complex interpersonal dynamics – proved invaluable in this role. My experiences as an older child prepared me to manage the intense scrutiny and high stakes of this position, reaffirming my commitment to social justice. I was subsequently awarded a formal letter of acknowledgement for my strategic leadership in the prison after Professor Guss John attended a regional HMP conference where my team and I presented our progress in addressing race within our local prison. As a Diversity Manager, my academic studies and lived experiences of racism, hostility, and gang attacks deeply shaped who I became—though much of this remained hidden beneath my Superwoman cape. These challenges quietly honed my resilience, sharpened my instincts, and deepened my understanding of the unwritten dynamics of human behaviour. I ran, using these hard-earned skills without openly sharing their origins or acknowledging the toll they had taken. My hypersensitivity, often perceived as a burden, became one of my greatest assets within the prison environment, enabling me to read subtle shifts in behaviour, body language, and atmosphere.

Working with violent and dangerous men demanded an acute awareness of subtle or sudden threats of attack, and this heightened sensitivity became an invisible shield, helping me navigate volatile situations with precision. It also allowed me to expect conflict and de-escalate tension before it erupted, fostering an environment of cautious trust. These experiences shaped my ability to critically analyse systemic inequalities, develop effective strategies, and lead with empathy, even in the most hostile environments. Yet, hidden under the guise of my cape, these skills were rarely acknowledged or celebrated. They were simply part of how I survived and excelled, quietly transforming my unique challenges into the tools that were effective.

Leadership Lessons from Prison Leadership and Management

1. **Empathy as a Tool for Influence**: Understanding and valuing the lived experiences of others, including prisoners and staff, fosters trust and creates a foundation for meaningful dialogue and change.
2. **Adaptability in High-Stakes Environments**: Leading in a volatile environment taught me to still be calm under

pressure, anticipate challenges, and respond swiftly to crises with clarity and confidence.

3. **The Power of Emotional Intelligence**: Navigating complex dynamics required heightened awareness of nonverbal cues, emotional undercurrents, and subtle shifts in behaviour, enabling me to de-escalate tensions and build rapport.

4. **Balancing Authority with Approachability**: Effective leadership involves asserting authority when necessary while staying approachable and fair to foster respect and cooperation.

5. **Strategic Thinking Amid Constraints**: Operating within a rigid system demanded creativity and critical thinking to develop strategies that addressed systemic inequities while achieving practical outcomes.

6. **The Importance of Self-Awareness**: Recognising my own triggers, biases, and strengths allowed me to lead authentically, set boundaries, and make decisions with integrity.

7. **Leading with Courage and Resilience**: Managing in an environment with overt risks and challenges reinforced the importance of standing firm in the face of adversity, while staying focused on long-term goals.

8. **Empowering Others**: Leadership is about empowering teams and individuals to take ownership of their roles, fostering a culture of accountability and shared success.

9. **Managing Relationships Across Differences**: Building productive relationships with a diverse range of stakeholders — including prison officers, governors, inspectors,

> prisoners, and their solicitors — required a nuanced approach to understanding different priorities, communication styles, and perspectives. Navigating these dynamics with professionalism and respect ensured alignment toward common goals and minimised conflict.

These lessons have not only shaped my leadership style but also reinforced the value of vulnerability, balance, and strategic vision in navigating complex and challenging environments.

White Fragility and Black Joy

Case Study: Marcia in the Workplace

> *Marcia, an office manager in a predominantly white organisation, watches as her colleague, Sarah, openly vents her frustrations in a meeting. Sarahs voice shakes, her eyes fill with tears, and she expresses how overwhelmed she feels. The room responds with concern — her manager offers to reduce her workload, and another colleague suggests a team lunch to boost morale Later that week, Marcia, facing mounting pressures and unrealistic expectations, finally breaks down in a one-on-one with her manager. Unlike Sarah, her tears are met with discomfort. She is asked if she is coping and subtly reminded of the need for professionalism. A few days later, she overhears whispers about whether she is too emotional for leadership. The contrast is stark — while Sarah's vulnerability is rewarded with support, Marcia is framed as a liability. The unspoken rule becomes clear: Marcia must suppress her emotions to be seen as competent, even at the cost of her own health and well-being.*

During my journey of liberation, I often found myself questioning whether I was free. As a Black woman navigating white-dominated spaces, I became acutely aware of the intricate dynamics of power, privilege and patriarchy that permeated environments. The struggle to feel emotionally safe has been a constant challenge throughout my career. In my pursuit of 'staying in my own lane', I frequently ran roughshod over my own emotions, becoming so busy tending to the needs of others that I neglected my own well-being and Reflecting on the old black-and-white film *Gone with the Wind*, particularly the character who won an Oscar for portraying the "mammy" figure, I began to recognise my own pattern of self-silencing. It was a form of self-preservation—a strategy I unconsciously adopted to navigate spaces where I often felt outnumbered and, at times, invisible. I noticed that some of my white women colleagues often displayed what scholar and author Robin DiAngelo terms *white fragility*—a defensive reaction that emerges when white people are confronted with or made aware of racial inequality and their own racial privilege. DiAngelo, a sociologist known for her work on whiteness and critical racial consciousness, explains that this fragility often shows up as discomfort, defensiveness, or even hostility when their social position is challenged, even in subtle ways.

This added another layer of complexity to my leadership experience, as I navigated the fine line between asserting my identity and role along with managing the delicate sensibilities of those around me. The juxtaposition of their fragility against my own need to constantly prove my worth was both frustrating and exhausting. It underscored the harsh reality that liberation is not a destination but a continuous journey, one that requires ongoing reflection and resilience in the face of deeply ingrained societal structures.

Reflecting on the notion of power and privilege, I have often observed in wonder how white women often move through spaces within systems, albeit conscious or unconscious, using power and privilege to express both their joy and sadness openly, shedding tears without the weight of cultural expectations that dictate composure. For Black women, tears — if shed in public — can be seen as weakness or even weaponised against us, exposing the power dynamics that differentiate our realities. Many one-to-one conversations over the years across different organisations and systems have reinforced the notion of feeling unsafe and sitting through white women colleagues who run out of meetings in floods of tears across all levels of leadership and management not always against the Black women but the open demonstration of emotion throughout my leadership career. I am struggling to recount on one hand how many Black women I have witnessed publicly or privately break down, relegating the Black woman into an unsafe, hostile environment and labelled as the troublemaker. In my professional experience, the tears of a Black woman can be dangerous to her, yet tears can be healing.

This manipulation of the victim-perpetrator dynamic exemplifies DiAngelo's critique of white fragility and its role in perpetuating systemic racism. It also underscores a critical challenge for Black women in leadership: the lack of psychological safety in workplaces where their voices and experiences are routinely dismissed.

In many workplaces, white women's frustration, anger, and tears are often met with sympathy, concern, and validation. Their visible distress can prompt immediate action, accommodations, or even career advantages. This response is deeply tied to power and privilege — white women's emotions are often perceived as humanising, reinforcing narratives of vulnerability that elicit protection and support. In contrast, when a Black woman expresses similar emotions — whether frustration, exhaustion, or anger — she is often met with discomfort, dismissal, or punishment. She is labelled as aggressive, difficult, or lacking professionalism. This disparity forces Black women to suppress their emotions, leading to internalised stress and contributing to significant health disparities, particularly during menopause, when hormonal fluctuations can heighten emotional responses. Without safe spaces to release this burden, Black women carry the weight of unspoken frustrations, increasing their risk of hypertension, cardiovascular disease, and mental health struggles. Creating dedicated spaces for Black women to express themselves without fear of judgement is not a luxury but a necessity for their well-being and longevity.

I was always aware of how some white male prison officers would seek validation from Black male colleagues about having a Black woman as their leader — as if they needed reassurance that my authority was legitimate. It was a subtle but clear attempt to undermine my leadership, testing whether I had the backing of Black men before they decided how to respond to me. This dynamic added another layer to white fragility, where their discomfort wasn't about race, but also about gender and power.

5 Reflective Points for Black Women

1. Where can you safely express your emotions without fear of judgment?

2. How do workplace power dynamics impact how your emotions are perceived?

3. What coping strategies can you implement to safeguard your mental and physical health?

4. Who in your network understands your experiences and can provide genuine support?

5. What boundaries can you set to prioritise your well-being over harmful workplace expectations?

Chapter Summary

The emotional double standard in the workplace leaves Black women with little room to express frustration, grief, or exhaustion without negative consequences. While white women's emotions are often met with care, Black women risk being labelled unprofessional for expressing the same feelings. This suppression has long-term health consequences, particularly during menopause, when hormonal changes make emotional regulation even more challenging. Safe spaces — both within and outside work — are crucial for Black women to process their experiences without fear of retribution. Recognising and addressing these disparities is essential not just for workplace equality but for the health and longevity of Black women.

Joy and Laughter

From my earliest memories, there was always something deeply reassuring about the sound of a Black woman's laughter. As a child, it felt like a lullaby—familiar, grounding, and powerful. When a Black woman laughs, she doesn't just make a sound; her whole body joins in. It's in the way her shoulders shake, her head tilts back, and her arms lift—sometimes outstretched as though gathering us all in an embrace. Her laughter fills a room, not just with joy, but with history, resistance, and a quiet kind of triumph. There was—and still is—a sacredness in that sound. It reminds me of where I come from, and the women whose joy carried us forward.

As a child the sound of a mother's laughter interwoven with the joyous cackles of a group of elderly Black women was the purest signifier of safety. Their laughter filled our home, a stark contrast to the often-unspoken struggles and challenges of their daily lives. In those moments, the world outside seemed to vanish, replaced by a sanctuary of mirth and camaraderie, fun and laughter. The rich, melodic tones of their joy conveyed stories untold, of resilience and strength, but in those instances, it was the laughter itself that spoke volumes. It was a stark reminder that even amid adversity, there could be moments of unadulterated happiness and togetherness. It gave me a sense of psychological safety.

Or overhearing Black women speak on how hard life was working, experiencing discrimination at work, in the street when going about their daily business minding their own business and so to hear a Black woman laugh was a kind of music signalling safety, and this tended to be on a Sunday after church when we would visit their Jamaican families or we would have visitors. The men would play dominoes in the back room and we would be in the kitchen cooking, and music would be blaring out from the 'best room', where the large radio player with the crocheted doily and dry flowers in a crystal vase would be moved to the side so that we could change the albums.

At this early stage of the book, I am giving you a health warning. For anyone who has felt the weight of wearing their Superwoman cape and they are now ready to free themselves from it, I heed caution. This is not an action to be taken lightly. I burnt my cape several years ago. The feeling of no longer wearing it left me feeling exposed, and also excited about my future. I was free! I had liberated myself and was finally showing up as my true, authentic, Black, beautiful, healthy self to the world. Yes, I felt vulnerable, but I knew that I no longer wished to investigate a world through the lenses of limiting beliefs and hopelessness. My ancestors have made too many sacrifices to see me live in a state of hopelessness – of which, I am sure. I have found my voice; I am finally showing up as ME. In the work by Bell Hooks, *Talking Back: Thinking Feminist, Thinking Black*, she explores the intersection of feminism and Blackness, highlighting the experiences and perspectives of Black women within feminist movements. Hooks discusses the complexities of identity, power and dynamics, and the struggle for liberation faced by Black women in society marked by racism, sexism, and classism. She critiques mainstream feminist movements for often excluding or marginalising Black women's voices and experiences, advocating for a more inclusive and intersectional approach to feminism.

Let us begin with defining the notion of Superwoman syndrome through the lens of the Black woman. The term originated from Dr Cheryl L. Woods-Giscombe, a professor at the Chapel University of North Carolina School of Nursing, who created it to describe the multiple levels of oppression experienced by many Black women in their attempt to juggle multiple obligations, such as caregiving, maybe studying and working to maintain responsible leadership management roles while navigating societal expectations and systemic challenges. Black women in society are viewed as the Mammy or the Mule, often at the expense of their own health and well-being, continuing to be self-sacrificing, resilient.

Discovering My Identity: "Who Do You Think You Are?"

If I were to give a penny to every person in my life who has said, "Who do you think you are?" to me, I would be a rich woman. In my younger years I had to be very creative on my route to the local corner shop as there would always be a gang of white girls who would be ready to ambush me and circle me on my way to the local corner shop, and the sneering racist remarks would ring in my ears, with one of those quotes being, "Who do you think you are?" The elderly white men would be particularly abusive, feeling the need to accost little Beverley and angrily tell her that, "We fought the war for you a lot." This was a quote which has often played as bell chiming in my ears: "Who do I think I am?"

Leadership Life Lessons:

Education Awareness.
- Policy development: Advocate for policy development, changes, and reforms that address systemic inequalities and discrimination based on skin colour. Support efforts to promote equity and social justice for all individuals, regardless of skin tone.

- Challenge discriminatory practices.

- Embrace diversity.

- Self-love empowerment.

- Support affected communities.

Chapter 4
DOUBLE THE STRUGGLE

"Out of many, one people"
Jamaican proverb

Shades of Trouble: Double the Struggle Confronting the Challenges of Colourism.

In this chapter I delve into the complex and pervasive issues of colourism, exploring how societal attitudes toward skin colour impact on the lives of Black women. Through personal insights and analysis, I cover the harmful effects of colourism on self-esteem, opportunities, and relationships, while also discussing strategies for resilience and empowerment in the face of this enduring challenge.

The first-generation Jamaican Black woman embodies a legacy of resilience and selfishness, prioritising family, and domestic responsibilities above personal needs. Growing up seeing this steadfast dedication, I unwittingly internalised the ethos of sacrifice, adopting my own version of the Superwoman cape as a survival strategy. As a child I was forever reminded.

Black Women Role Models

Back in the day before the Race Relations Act came about, as a little girl I never saw a Black woman featured on the front cover of a magazine.

Apart from my immediate family, I was never exposed to positive Black women role models. My understanding back then from marketing experts was that featuring a Black woman on the front cover of a magazine produced a dip in sales.

Roll forward to 2024 and I have since seen, heard and met many wonderful powerful Black woman role models who are continuing to motivate, empower and inspire.

This cape woven with threads of strength and determination shields against adversities while propelling forward in the pursuit of dreams.

It is a testament to generations of women who navigated complexity with grace, embodying resilience, and fortitude in every stride.

Yet, amid the strength lies a journey of self-discovery, recognising the need for self-care and balance of empowerment and fulfilment. The evolution from inheriting a legacy to shaping one's narrative is a testament to resilience and the power of reclaiming one's identity while honouring ancestral wisdom.

When a Black woman finds herself under fire — whether from societal pressures, systemic challenges, or personal adversities — she often carries herself with a remarkable grace. Grace, in this context, encompasses resilience, dignity, and strength in the face of adversity. It is a multifaceted quality that enables Black women to navigate tricky situations, cultural heritage, and a history of overcoming immense challenges. It empowers the Black women to assert their worth, demand respect, and inspire others through their actions and words, and unwavering commitment to justice and equity. Grace becomes not just a personal trait but also a powerful tool for resilience, empowerment, and effecting positive change in their communities and beyond, with poise, wisdom, and a steadfast resolve. Grace allows them to maintain their composure, even in moments of intense scrutiny or injustice, and respond with clarity and purpose rather than react impulsively. This ability to embody grace is rooted in a deep sense of self-awareness.

In conclusion, while both Black and white women may face challenges with grace, the impact on health and well-being is often more severe and complex for Black women due to the systematic inequalities, societal expectations, access to barriers, and intersectional identities. Addressing these disparities requires comprehensive efforts, including dismantling systemic racism, promoting mental health awareness and support, improving access to health and resources, and fostering inclusive and supportive environments for all women facing adversity.

Here is a critical analysis of these differences:

- **Societal Expectations**: Black women often face compounded societal expectations and pressures due to intersectional identities, including race, gender, disability, and sexual orientation. These expectations can include the "The Strong Black Woman" which can idealise strength and resilience at the expense of vulnerability and self-care. In contrast, white women may encounter expectations that may not place as much emphasis without showing vulnerability.

- **Perceived Discrimination and Microaggressions**: Black women are more likely to experience discrimination and microaggressions due to their lived experience at the intersection of race and gender, making them more attuned to subtle forms of bias and exclusion.

Access to Resources: Structural inequalities and systemic racism can limit access to resources such as healthcare, mental health support, and socio-economic opportunities for Black women. This lack of access can exacerbate stressors and negatively impact on overall health outcomes compared with white women facing similar challenges who may have greater access to resources and support networks.

Unfurling the Superwoman Cape:
Pioneering Cultural Transformation

The Black Woman's Journey to Joy and Laughter, Self-Care, and Rest

My transition from wearing my Superwoman cape to a focus on myself has proved to be such a transformative season of rediscovery and self-care. In this period, I have dedicated time to nurturing joy and laughter, recognising their profound impact on my mental and emotional well-being. Prioritising self-care has become non-negotiable, allowing me to recharge and cultivate a healthier relationship with my whole self. Rest, often overlooked in the rush of everyday life, has emerged as a cornerstone of this journey, providing the necessary space for reflection, growth, and inner peace. This intentional focus on self has not only replenished my energy but also deepened my understanding of "doing the work" and the importance of balance and resilience, essential elements for navigating life's myriad challenges with renewed vigour, grace, and strength.

Practical Tools and Tips:

1. Set boundaries develop and strengthen your "No" muscle to tasks which drain you of your energy or do not align with your priorities. Establishing boundaries helps protect your time and mental well-being.

2. Schedule me time block out regular periods in your daily schedule dedicated solely to activities that bring you joy, relaxation, and rejuvenation. Evaluate this time as non-negotiable self-care appointments.

3. Delegate responsibilities: do not hesitate to delegate tasks at work or home to trusted individuals. Recognise that asking for help is not a sign of strength and not weakness.

4. Develop a mindfulness practice. Incorporate mindfulness practice such as meditation, deep breathing, or mindful walking into your daily routine. These can help to reduce stress and increase self-awareness.

5. Prioritise sleep: aim for at least hours.

Stepping into The Spotlight

Navigating Workplace Solitude: The Challenges of Being the Only Black woman

"When I look at you, I don't see your colour. I treat everyone the same."

As I reflect over a 40-year plus working career and my varied roles across different complex bureaucratic systems, I cannot count the number of times that this statement has been said to me.

In the face of persistent statements like this, it is vital that systems acknowledge the erasure of identity and the dismissal of unique experiences for Black women navigating white spaces, that true inclusion means being seen and heard authentically, not just as a token of diversity and inclusion.

The perpetuation of statements continues a harmful myth of 'colour blindness' that undermines the reality of systemic inequalities and their impact on health outcomes.

To what extent are we genuinely recognising and taking action to address these disparities and, in doing so, truly fostering a sense of belonging?

Through observations over the years, my own experiences and coaching Black women, many of them fear the spotlight in professional settings due to the pervasive invalidation which they have experienced within systems when invitations feel more like token gestures than genuine recognition of their talents.

An invitation to enter the spotlight becomes a daunting reminder of the pressure to perform exceptionally, and often heightened scrutiny, while often, the voice and perspectives of the Black woman are still sidelined. Such wounds can cut deep and take time to heal.

It reinforces the fear of being reduced to a mere diversity checkbox. This cycle of invalidation can perpetuate a reluctance to step into the spotlight or speak up, knowing that we are measured by a different yardstick. True acceptance and acknowledgement for the Black woman can remain elusive within existing structures. I applaud every Black woman who has refused to dim their light. Your bright light will help those who look to confidently shine theirs.

I have learned that psychological safety is not a nice-to-have but a fundamental necessity for any high-performing, diverse team. Throughout my experiences, particularly when collaborating with women of colour and exploring how the imposter syndrome intersects with race and identity, I have seen how vital it is for every team member to feel seen, heard and valued.

Enabling the Black Woman to Move from Surviving to Thriving
Creating psychological safety in the corporate workplace is essential to enable and empower Black women. Here are five key strategies that can help foster a supportive and inclusive environment:

Open Dialogue and Active Listening: Encourage open conversations about diversity, equity, and inclusion. Create spaces where Black women feel comfortable sharing their experiences and concerns. Active listening from leadership and peers is crucial to validate their voices and address any issues.

Mentorship and Sponsorship Programs: Establish mentorship and sponsorship programs specifically for Black women. Having mentors and sponsors who advocate for their growth, development, and career advancement can provide essential support and open opportunities.

Bias Training and Awareness: Implement regular bias training to educate employees about unconscious biases and microaggressions. Raising awareness and providing tools to address these issues can help create a more respectful and inclusive workplace culture.

Inclusive Policies and Practices: Develop and enforce policies that promote diversity and inclusion. This includes fair hiring practices, equal pay, opportunities for advancement, and ensuring representation at all levels of the organisation. Make it clear that discrimination and harassment will not be tolerated.

Employee Resource Groups (ERGs): Support the formation of ERGs for Black women and other underrepresented groups. These groups provide a safe space for networking, sharing experiences, and advocating for changes within the company. They also help build a sense of community and belonging.

Organisational Benefits: a Focused Strategy to Support Black Women

Supporting a strategy that empowers and supports Black women can bring numerous benefits for an organisation. Here are seven benefits:

Enhanced Diversity and Inclusion: Organisations that prioritise diversity and inclusion are more likely to attract and retain a diverse talent pool. This can lead to a more innovative and dynamic workplace where different perspectives and ideas are valued.

Improved Employee Morale and Engagement: When Black women feel supported and valued, their morale and engagement levels increase. This can lead to higher job satisfaction, increased productivity, and a more positive work environment for all employees.

Greater Talent Retention: By fostering an inclusive culture, organisations can reduce turnover rates among Black women and other underrepresented groups. This saves costs associated with recruitment and training and ensures that valuable talent remains within the company.

Enhanced Reputation and Brand Image: Companies that demonstrate a commitment to diversity and inclusion are often viewed more favourably by customers, clients, and the public. This can enhance the organisations reputation, attract a broader customer base, and strengthen brand loyalty.

Better Decision-Making and Problem-Solving: Diverse teams bring a variety of perspectives and experiences to the table. This can lead to more effective decision-making, innovative solutions, and improved problem-solving capabilities.

Compliance and Risk Management: Supporting diversity and inclusion initiatives helps organisations comply with legal and regulatory requirements related to equal employment opportunities. This can reduce the risk of discrimination claims and create a more equitable workplace.

Increased Competitive Advantage: Companies that embrace diversity and inclusion are often better positioned to compete in the global marketplace. They can leverage the unique strengths and talents of a diverse workforce to drive business success.

Creating psychological safety requires a concerted effort from the entire organisation, with leadership playing a pivotal role. By implementing these strategies, companies can foster an environment where Black women feel valued, empowered, and supported.

Leadership Life Lessons: Five Benefits of Laughter
For me, one of the best feelings is when I laugh so much that my tummy hurts! Research by Dr. Berk & Tan highlights that there are many positive health and well-being benefits of laughter:

- Lowers blood pressure and can decrease levels of inflammation.
- Reduces stress hormone levels.
- Can help improve cardiac health.
- Can help trigger the release of endorphins.
- Can help produce a sense of well-being.

Grieving Alone in the Kitchen

The lockdown transformed my home into both a sanctuary and a prison. Each morning, I sat at my kitchen table, staring into the stillness of a world paused, my grief growing louder in the silence. The 3 a.m. phone calls from relatives carried the same devastating refrain: another loved one had become an ancestor. I was alone, confined by the restrictions of the pandemic, unable to gather, unable to mourn as my culture dictated. Grieving in isolation, I unknowingly called upon survival skills I had developed over years of systemic challenges. They whispered reminders to endure, to keep going, even as my chest tightened with panic in the quiet of the night.

The Train of Panic—Anxiety Attacks

The first time it happened, I thought I was dying. My heart racing so fast it felt like it might burst. I dropped to the floor, clutching at the carpet, certain I would be found lifeless days later. Blue-lighted ambulances tore up and down the main road nearby, which heightened my attacks further. I didn't visit my GP; I felt that she was far too busy, and, during this time, it would have only been a telephone appointment, so my years of surviving kicked in. But this was something different and I didn't understand what was happening: panic attacks. They arrived without warning; a train of anxiety battling through my carefully curated exterior of my Black Superwoman cape and my image of calm and control. I needed another strategy to combat this new thing that was happening to me.

For a long time, I told no one. I feared being seen as weak, incapable of leading during a time when others depended on me. So, I managed the attacks in silence, swallowing the rising panic as I strategised solutions for the frontline clinical leaders I was charged with supporting. It was at this time, through research, that I discovered the menopause and loss of oestrogen, poor sleep could be contributory factors to my panic attacks. But what next?

Leading Through Cultural Blindness

The pandemic's toll on Black and brown lives was not a surprise to many of us. Long before the data became headlines, we knew the inequities that shaped our communities. But the systemic failures that emerged during this time were staggering. Support systems existed in theory but often lacked the cultural nuance and understanding to make them effective. Many leaders, well-intentioned but uninformed, offered solutions rooted in a one-size-fits-all approach that only deepened the chasm of inequity.

It became clear to me that cultural incompetence was itself a silent pandemic — one that had quietly claimed lives long before C19 arrived. The work I led was not just about responding to immediate clinical needs; it was about demanding systemic change, amplifying the voices of those who had been ignored, and shining a light on the overlooked intersections of race, health, and care.

Finding Resilience in the Rubble
Though I grieved and suffered in silence, my inner wisdom told me that resilience is not about ignoring pain but about finding strength amid it. As the walls of my home closed in, I leaned into resilience tools I had unknowingly forged over a lifetime of navigating spaces that were not designed for me — and yet I showed up.

I rediscovered the power of boundaries, learning to say no without guilt as I carved out moments of rest and stillness. I sought out Black joy wherever it could be found — through virtual connections with loved ones, through moments of humour amid heaviness, and through a deep, intentional focus on self-preservation.

Leadership Life Lessons From Under My Superwoman Cape
In times of crisis, I learned the following:

- Lead from a place of self-love and humanity rather than martyrdom.
- Acknowledgement that a Black woman leader does not require one to be invincible.

- **Vulnerability is Strength:** Admitting when I was struggling allowed others to do the same, fostering an environment of honesty and collective healing.

Rest is Revolutionary:

The world will not collapse if you stop for a moment to breathe. Leadership thrives when leaders are whole.

Burning the Superwoman cape was not about giving up — it was about reclaiming myself. It was about leading with authenticity and reminding others that even amid fear, anxiety, and grief, resilience is possible. Through it all, I learned that the strongest leaders are those who can stand tall without a cape, rooted in the knowledge of their humanity.

Chapter 5
REINVENTION:
Burning My Superwoman Cape,

"Who does she think she is?"

For more years than I care to mention, I had been thwarted in my own attempts to show up authentically in a Black woman's body in a world of whiteness. It's a world where the white body and its beauty standards access equitable health outcomes and the education and criminal justice systems hold more currency than those of the Black body. My Superwoman cape functioned as an enabler to hide, and to try to absorb and assimilate. Over the years I observed white bodies showing up as their authentic selves in all spaces of society. The white body had a true sense of belonging. My Superwoman cape had its limitations, and as I got older the cape was drawing heavy. It was exhausting, weathering, and I was losing who I was.

There are many definitions of Superwoman. Here are some of them: strong, powerful, resilient, fearless, a warrior, dependable, empathetic to others, smiley, happy. In a world of power, privilege, and whiteness, the Black body is often required to be all things to all people. My Superwoman cape was stitched with threads captured from systems, threads of oppression, racism, aggression, bullying, discrimination, violence, tone police, and overlocked stitching around my cape of misogynoir.

My story provides a unique perspective of a second-generation Jamaican/Black British child raised in Greater Manchester, navigating the complexities of identity, culture, and opportunity within the north of England. My story is set against heritage and multiculturalism. This book offers a compelling narrative which explores the nuances of being Black British outside London. However, despite the geographical differences, my book uncovered striking commonalities shared by Black women in leadership roles, as they navigate through large, bureaucratic systems. This book highlights the resilience, creativity, and determination of Black women in carving out their paths within institutional frameworks, fostering a deeper understanding of their experiences and contributions to society.

Through extensive research and personal reflections, I have come to recognise the detrimental effects of not working through one's emotions, especially in high-stress environments such as the corporate world of the public sector.

When Abundance Felt Like a Threat

There was a time in my life when I believed I had to fight for every inch. Not because I wasn't capable — I've always known I had something special — but because I was raised in environments where survival was the goal. Where money was tight, time was tighter, and space to dream felt like a luxury only others had. That scarcity taught me to hustle, to be grateful for scraps, and never expect too much. It was a mindset built on lack — lack of rest, lack of choice, lack of safety and, sometimes, lack of self-worth. I wore my strength like armour and stitched my Superwoman cape out of all the "nos" I'd heard in life. I kept it on even when it choked me.

So, when abundance finally came — when I moved into my dream home, when I found myself booking holidays abroad that I used to only hear other people talk about, when I walked into rooms I used to admire from a distance — I didn't know how to receive it. I questioned it. Was it real? Was it earned? Was it a mistake? I'd spent so long surviving that thriving felt foreign. Like a trick, a trap.

The truth is that abundance triggered my imposter syndrome in ways I wasn't ready for. My mind whispered, *"You don't belong here,"* even as my heart knew I'd worked damn hard to arrive. And instead of embracing my softness, my joy, my rest — I doubled down. Cape on. Smile fixed. Pushing through. Performing excellence.

But here's what I had to learn: abundance is not a threat. It's a birthright. And I was not an imposter — I was a woman finally walking into what she deserved, and what had been waiting for her all along. I didn't need to keep proving, performing, or protecting myself from goodness. I just needed to open my hands, drop the cape, and allow myself to receive.

Reclaiming my rest meant unlearning scarcity. It meant teaching my nervous system that safety and success can co-exist. That joy isn't dangerous. I don't need to *earn* peace — I can *choose* it.

That's when everything began to shift. Not just in my career, but in my spirit and the following three strategies was what enabled me to push forward and remain future focused:

1. Adopting manifestation techniques.

2. Self-talk positive affirmation looking in the mirror.

3. Regular and intentional journaling.

Reflection Prompt:

Think of a time when something good came into your life—a win, a breakthrough, or a long-held dream finally coming true. Did you allow yourself to fully receive it? Or did imposter syndrome creep in?

- What did you feel in that moment?

- What old stories about scarcity or not being enough were still echoing in your mind?

- How can you begin to trust abundance and rest in the knowledge that you deserve the life you have built?

What I Say to Myself About Myself

I have spent decades unravelling the coded language of my own self-talk.

The whispers I used to internalise were not mine alone. They were shaped by the echoes of a Britain that saw me through a lens of invisibility, hyper-visibility, or both — but rarely humanity. Born in the 1960s, I inherited more than my grandmother's cheekbones or my mother's resilience. I inherited a legacy of caution. Of survival. Of silence. And woven into that legacy were messages about what a Black woman *should* be — obedient, strong, silent, grateful, unbreakable.

It took me years — and a Master's degree in diversity strategic management, grounded in Black feminist scholarship and the psychology of self-concept — to see the full picture: that the conversations we have with ourselves are not just personal. They are political. They are historical. They are generational.

The Language We Inherit

As a young girl, I learned that being "too loud", "too clever", or "too sensitive" could draw the wrong kind of attention. That hair like mine needed "taming". That my worth was tethered to how well I conformed to someone else's expectations. These weren't just family lessons; they were societal instructions. And like many daughters of the diaspora, I carried them with me into school, into work, and eventually into leadership.

What I said to myself mirrored what society had already whispered: *Don't make mistakes. Don't ask for too much. Don't take up space.*

This is the soundtrack of Black women's imposter syndrome — not the false humility of high-achievers, but the well-earned doubt that comes from navigating systems that question our legitimacy before we even speak.

Rewriting the Script

I remember sitting in supervision, mentoring a younger Black woman who said, "Sometimes I feel like I'm acting at work. Like I've fooled everyone." I recognised that script immediately – it was one I had memorised years before. The difference was, I'd since begun the challenging work of unlearning it.

Black psychologists such as Dr Joy DeGruy and Dr Thema Bryant have long explored the psychological impact of internalised oppression and the power of self-affirmation. Dr DeGruy's research into post-traumatic slave syndrome helped me understand that some of our inner dialogue – especially around competence, beauty, and value – is not a personal failing but a generational inheritance.

What I came to realise – through study and lived experience – is that imposter syndrome in Black women is not a personality flaw. It is often a coping mechanism, a survival tool in institutions where we were never meant to thrive. But survival is different from flourishing.

Coaching the Self First

In my coaching practice and in leadership workshops, I often ask: *What do you say to yourself about yourself?*

At first, many Black women whom I coached find this question confronting. But eventually, the answers start to surface. "I say I'm not ready." "I say I have to work twice as hard." "I say I don't belong in that room."

And when I ask, "Whose voice is that?" – the shift begins.

I have learned that this work of excavating and reauthoring our inner dialogue is not just personal development. It is resistance. It is liberation. Through structured reflection, journaling, and coaching exercises, I've helped many women replace their old scripts with new truths: *I am prepared. I bring value. I belong here.*

And I have had to do that work too — looking in the mirror and declaring, without flinching, *I am enough. I am more than my productivity. I am worthy of rest and joy.*

Leadership Lessons Learned

We must create new scripts — not borrowed from corporate speak or Instagram affirmations, but rooted in our truth, our culture, and our lived experience. I have learnt that reframing what I held about myself has been a game changer.

Reflection and Journaling Exercise: Reclaiming Your Inner Voice

"I am not what I was told I had to be. I am who I choose to become."

Take a moment to reflect. Find a quiet space. Breathe deeply. Then write freely, without judgement, using the prompts below.

1. **What do I say to myself about myself when no one else is listening?**
   Write down your most common inner thoughts. Be honest. What tone do they take — encouraging, critical, doubting?

2. **Whose voice is that?**
   Is it a parent? A teacher? A manager? A cultural narrative? Trace the origin. Does it belong to you, or did you inherit it?

3. **What belief about yourself are you ready to let go of?**
   Write it down. Then write a new belief to replace it. Example: "I have to prove myself every day" becomes "I am enough, and I bring value wherever I go."

4. **How has your self-talk shaped your leadership, your joy, or your rest?**
   Reflect on the ways your internal dialogue has influenced your decisions, relationships, or career path.

5. **What do you want the next generation of Black women to say to themselves?**
   Write a short message as if you were speaking to your younger self — or a future leader who needs your wisdom.

Leadership Life Lessons

Acquire an accredited coach with proven specialism in social justice, diversity equality and inclusion, or gender namely women of colour.

The removal of your Superwoman cape after many years can be incredibly challenging, as your hidden emotions or traumas may start to rise from under your superwoman cape. Consider seeking professional support as appropriate. Once again, as a woman of colour, it would be beneficial to work with someone who has proven expertise and understanding of what it can be like to navigate your new terrain once your cape has gone.

Understanding intersectionality: It is important that the coach has an awareness of the unique challenges which face Black women in the workplace which could amplify imposter syndrome.

Creating Safe Space: Foster an environment of trust and openness where Black women can feel comfortable exploring her experiences of self-doubt without judgement.

Challenging Stereotypes: Help the Black omen identify and challenge internalised and externalised stereotypes that contribute to imposter syndrome, emphasising her strengths and achievements.

Setting Realistic Goals: Collaborate on setting achievable goals and milestones, emphasising progress rather than perfection.

Provide Feedback: Offer constructive feedback which highlights strengths and areas for growth, promoting self-confidence and self-awareness.

Leadership Life Lessons for Black Woman

Embrace Authenticity: Recognise that vulnerability and imperfection are part of being human and a leader, authenticity builds trusts and connection with others.

Seek Mentorship and Support: Build a network of Mentors, Sponsors, and Peers who can provide guidance, feedback and support in navigating challenges and opportunities.

Celebrate Achievements: Acknowledge and celebrate your accomplishments and milestones, no matter how small, to counteract feelings of inadequacy.

Continuous learning: Embrace growth mindset and prioritise ongoing learning and development to expand skills and knowledge.

Self-Care: Create and maintain a personal self-self-care practice that serves your emotional, physical, and mental well-being, recognising that self-care is essential for sustainable leadership.

Leadership and Management Tips for the White Manager

Psychological Safety

As I reflect on my management and leadership career across large-scale organisations and within commercial settings from the world several. Much has been said and researched on the concept of psychological safety by Amy Edmonson.

Cultural Awareness: Educate yourself on cultural differences and biases that may impact your perceptions and interactions with Black women in the workplace.

Three Scenarios for Critical Reflection or Discussion. The following case studies have been designed to facilitate thoughtful dialogue and critical thinking, helping readers or workshop participants explore the dynamics of race culture and psychological safety.

Scenario 1: Navigating Cultural Blind Spots During a Global Crisis

During a global outbreak, a healthcare team faced unprecedented challenges while managing frontline operations. Black staff members, who were disproportionately exposed to risks, expressed concerns about safety protocols. They felt that senior leadership lacked cultural understanding and were unable to make nuanced risk assessments that accounted for systemic disparities.

When a Black staff member requested reassignment from direct patient contact due to vulnerability, their concerns were dismissed. Meanwhile, other team members were reassigned without question, leaving the Black staff feeling unsupported and unsafe.

Discussion Questions:

What factors may have contributed to the senior leader's inability to recognise and address the concerns of Black staff?

How can organisations ensure that risk assessments are inclusive and culturally sensitive, especially during crises?

What steps could the leadership team take to foster a sense of psychological safety for Black staff in such high-stakes situations?

Reflection Exercise:

Imagine you are a team leader during this crisis. What actions would you take to address these concerns? How would you create a safe space for staff to raise sensitive issues?

Scenario 2: The Weekend Check-In Challenge

In a small, white team, weekly check-ins included sharing weekend activities to build camaraderie. While most team members eagerly participated, two Black staff members rarely contributed. They appeared hesitant and reserved, which led to their colleagues perceiving them as disengaged.

However, the reluctance to share stemmed from feeling culturally isolated and fearing judgment or microaggressions about their personal lives. The informal nature of these check-ins, intended to build connection, inadvertently highlighted cultural gaps within the team.

Discussion Questions:

What might prevent someone from feeling safe enough to share personal experiences in a team setting?

How could unspoken power dynamics or cultural differences contribute to this reluctance?

What could the team or its leader do to create a more inclusive and psychologically safe environment for all members?

Reflection Exercise:
Reflect on a time when you felt hesitant to share in a group setting. What would have helped you feel more comfortable? How can you apply this understanding to foster inclusivity in your own teams?

Example 3: Advocating for Inclusion in Decision-Making

Yvonne worked in an organisation where decisions were often made in informal, exclusive networks. Although she held a high-ranking position, she frequently found herself excluded from key discussions. When she finally confronted the issue, she was met with defensiveness, with colleagues insisting the exclusion was "unintentional".

Yvonne advocated for a formalised decision-making process that ensured all key stakeholders were included. Over time, this shift not only improved her sense of belonging but also enhanced the organisation's overall transparency and fairness.

Reflection:
Exclusion, even if unintentional, undermines psychological safety by reinforcing feelings of invisibility and undervaluation.

Insight for Leaders:
To foster psychological safety, organisations must address informal power dynamics and ensure equitable representation in all decision-making processes. This requires intentionality, transparency, and consistent practices that uphold fairness.

Unmasking Authentic Leadership: Passing on the Legacy Beyond the Superwoman Cape

In my journey to finally burn my Superwoman cape and embrace my true, authentic self, I have often reflected on the wise words of ancestors such as when someone shows you who they are, believe them the first time. This resonates with me deeply as, throughout my working career, I have encountered many challenges in professional relationships where, at first, I chose to overlook certain behaviour and signals as my Superwoman cape functioned as a shield and where I chose to view such behaviour in many circumstances as isolated incidents or misunderstandings. However, as time moved on, those initial signs proved to be accurate indicators of a person's true character and intentions. Maya Angelou's message holds profound significance for Black women in leadership roles, reminding us to trust our instincts, observe actions over words, and set boundaries based on respect and integrity. It is a powerful reminder to prioritise self-awareness, discernment, and authenticity in navigating professional relationships and leadership responsibilities, empowering us to cultivate environments of trust, accountability, and mutual respect.

Burning the Cape to Lead Authentically: Rejecting the "Good Girl" Myth

"The Good Girl Never Gets the Corner Office"

The phrase *"The good girl never gets the corner office"* is a reminder that following the rules and playing it safe rarely leads to real success, especially in environments designed to maintain the status quo. For Black women navigating white-dominated spaces, this idea takes on a deeper meaning. Being the "good girl" often means conforming to behaviours that make others comfortable — being agreeable, staying quiet, and suppressing cultural identity. While this might help avoid conflict, it comes at a cost. Trying to fit into these expectations can erase who you are, separating you from the richness of your Blackness and the community that sustains you.

As a Black woman with over thirty-five years in leadership roles, rejecting the "good girl" mould has never meant being difficult or combative – it has simply meant choosing authenticity. It means leading with your voice, prioritising your boundaries, and defining success on your own terms. This choice is not an easy one, but it is freeing. My own lesson learned over the years has been to recognise my power and let go of the pressure to try to fit into spaces not designed for women of colour and instead focus on creating new spaces that honour our values and identities.

Here are three reflective questions for Black women:
- In what ways have you felt pressured to fit into spaces that were not designed for you, and how have you navigated those challenges?
- How do you define success on your own terms, and what boundaries do you need to set to honour that definition?
- What steps can you take to embrace your authenticity and create spaces that align with your values and identity?

Leadership Tips for Black Women Who Lead.
- **Redefine Success**
  Success is not about fitting into someone else's mold. Define what leadership looks like for you and prioritise goals that reflect your values and culture.

- **Lead Authentically**
  Embrace your unique voice and story. Authentic leadership inspires others and creates space for real change.

- **Set Boundaries**
Protect your time and energy. Boundaries are essential for maintaining joy and avoiding burnout.

- **Build Your Tribe**
Surround yourself with people who affirm and celebrate your identity, both inside and outside your workplace.

- **Celebrate Black Joy**
Incorporate joy and rest into your leadership journey. You do not have to carry the weight of the world to make an impact.

Reclaiming My Joy, Love, and Light

For much of my career, I was conditioned to believe that success meant constant striving — always achieving, always proving, always excelling. But what was missing in those moments of relentless pursuit was an appreciation of joy, love, creativity, and my own accomplishments. These are not indulgences; they are the very essence of what sustains us.

Moments of Joy and Love

As Black women, we have been taught — subtly and overtly — that shining too brightly can be dangerous. Historically, on the plantation, standing out could mean separation from family, increased scrutiny, or even punishment. That history lingers in our collective consciousness, shaping how we navigate the world today. We learn to be excellent, but not 'too' excellent. We learn to celebrate privately, but not publicly. We learn that humility is survival.

For years, I internalised this. I tempered my achievements, ensuring they didn't appear too grand. I worked hard, but I rarely allowed myself to revel in success. But then I began to question: who benefits from me making myself small? The answer was clear — it wasn't me. It wasn't the women looking up to me. And it certainly wasn't my younger self, who had once dreamed so boldly.

I remember the first time I truly exhaled in my leadership journey. It was during a quiet evening after delivering a workshop where I had poured my heart into empowering women of colour to own their voices. As I stepped outside, the sky a deep indigo, I felt a wave of satisfaction. The warmth of the room, the resonance of shared experiences, and the tears of gratitude from participants filled me with something I had neglected for so long — joy. Not the fleeting joy of ticking off an achievement, but the deep, soul-nourishing joy of knowing my work had meaning.

Love, too, has been an anchor. It showed up in the form of mentors who saw me beyond the expectations placed upon me. It was in the embrace of friendships built in the margins; in the way my family celebrated my wins even when I downplayed them. Love surrounded me when I dared to step into spaces not designed for me and, when I faltered, it was love that reminded me to stand tall again.

Creativity as a Source of Renewal

Creativity has been both my refuge and my resistance. There were times when the weight of professional expectations threatened to strip me of the parts of myself that found joy in writing, storytelling, and even movement. I used to love journaling, but at one point, I stopped. It felt self-indulgent in a world where I was constantly measured by output and performance. Yet, creativity was where I found my voice again. Writing became an act of defiance and restoration – a way to articulate the depths of my experience on my own terms. It was in crafting speeches, curating workshops, and even experimenting with diverse ways to express my story that I realised creativity was never absent; I had just stopped giving myself permission to embrace it.

Accomplishments – Owning My Shine

For a long time, I dimmed my light, believing that humility meant making myself smaller. I underplayed my accomplishments, fearful of being seen as 'too much' or 'too ambitious'. But the truth is, I had every right to bask in my success. I had worked tirelessly, navigated challenges with grace, and built something meaningful. The turning point came when I stood on a stage at a national conference, and instead of minimising my journey, I claimed it. I spoke with authority about the work I had done, the change I had led, and the impact I had made. In that moment, I allowed myself to feel pride — not just for the accolades, but for the resilience, the sacrifices, and the courage it took to get there.

Reflective Section: Reclaiming and Amplifying Our Light

To my sisters, my brothers, my kin —

We have been conditioned to keep our light under a bushel, to minimise our achievements, to work twice as hard and then step back so as not to be 'too visible'. But I urge you: shine. Bask in the joy of your accomplishments. Celebrate your creativity. Do not let anyone, including yourself, diminish the beauty of your journey.

Brené Brown speaks about the power of simply showing up, about the courage it takes to be seen. But for us, as Black women, it must be more than just showing up — we must glow up. We must embrace self-love, not in competition with others, but as an act of resistance, of healing, of legacy-building. We must shine not only for ourselves but to illuminate the path for those who will come after us.

Reflective Actions to Consider:

Your accomplishments are not just personal wins; they are testimonies of survival, resilience, and brilliance. So, stand in your light, fully and unapologetically. You deserve to be here. You deserve to be seen. And you deserve joy in abundance.

Chapter 7
GOLDEN REST
a Black Woman's Journey to Renewal, Reparation, and Rediscovery

- Discovering and Owning My Vulnerability
- Transitioning Through the Menopause
- My IKIGAI
- Revisiting Identity
- forming Anger into Liberation Trans
- Embracing Retirement and Self-Permission

Discovering and Owning My Vulnerability

Case Study: Adebola's Silent Struggle.

Adebola, a senior manager in a predominantly white English team, had always prided herself on her resilience. But today had been particularly tough — microaggressions in meetings, her ideas overlooked, and an offhand comment about her "tone" that cut deep. By the time she reached her office, the weight of it all pressed down on her chest. She wanted to cry.

But she hesitated. Would her colleagues see her as weak? Would she confirm stereotypes about being "too emotional"? Instead, she took a deep breath, swallowed her tears, and carried on.

Later, in a one-to-one with her mentor, she finally let go. "I feel like I have to hold everything in," she admitted. Her mentor nodded. "Strength isn't about never crying. It's about knowing when to release and who to trust."

That conversation changed everything. Adebola sought out safer spaces — mentors, networks, and self-care rituals — that allowed her to process her emotions without shame. She learned that vulnerability wasn't a weakness but a quiet act of resistance in a world that expected her to always be 'strong.'

In the world of superheroes, vulnerability is often seen as a weakness. But in the real world, it is a strength that we need to embrace. It is okay not to be okay all the time. It is okay to ask for help. It is okay to admit that you are tired, that you are hurt, that you are human.

This chapter explores the concept of vulnerability and how it can lead to growth and self-discovery. It delves into personal stories of times when the superwoman cape felt too heavy to wear, and how these moments of vulnerability led to profound personal transformations.

Through sharing my own story, we learn that burning the Superwoman cape does not mean giving up: it means letting go of the unrealistic expectations we set for ourselves and embracing our authentic selves. It means understanding that it is okay to fall if we pick ourselves back up. It means realising that our worth is not defined by how much we can manage alone, but by how we rise after we fall.

Social scientist experts such as Brené Brown encourage us to be vulnerable and lean into demanding situations. While I acknowledge the work by Brené Brown, the notion of vulnerability and curiosity are universal concepts and, through the lens of Black women, such concepts are as complex as the experiences of the Black woman are unique and, therefore, we have faced unique and complex challenges, for example, generational and societal traumas and health inequalities, to name a few.

So, let us burn that Superwoman cape. Let us embrace our vulnerability. Let us be brave enough to be ourselves. Because, in the end, that is the most super thing we can do.

Transitioning Through the Menopause

Black women experience menopause differently due to a combination of biological, social, and systemic factors that impact their symptoms, healthcare access, and overall experience. Here's why focusing specifically on Black women leaders is critical:

1. More Severe and Prolonged Symptoms

Studies from the UK and US indicate that Black women experience menopause symptoms — especially hot flashes, night sweats, and sleep disturbances — more intensely and for a longer duration than white women. The Study of Women's Health Across the Nation (SWAN) found that Black women reported vasomotor symptoms for an average of 10.1 years, compared with 6.5 years for white women.

2. Healthcare Disparities and Systemic Bias

British research has shown that Black women are significantly less likely to be prescribed hormone replacement therapy (HRT). A 2024 University of Oxford study found that Black African women in England were 80 per cent less likely to receive HRT than white women, despite reporting more severe symptoms. This is due to systemic bias, cultural stigma, and a lack of culturally competent healthcare professionals.

3. The "Superwoman Schema" in Black Women Leaders

Black women leaders often carry the burden of 'Superwoman syndrome' — a cultural expectation to be strong, resilient, and self-sufficient, even when experiencing physical or emotional distress. This can lead to:

- **Delayed healthcare seeking**, as many Black women prioritise work and caregiving responsibilities.

- **Increased stress**, which exacerbates menopausal symptoms.

- **Workplace challenges**, where menopause intersects with racism, sexism, and ageism, creating unique career barriers.

4. Impact on Leadership and Career Progression

Menopause symptoms — when combined with workplace discrimination — can affect Black women's career longevity, confidence, and executive presence. A 2022 UK survey found that women of colour were twice as likely to consider leaving their jobs due to menopause symptoms but were less likely to feel comfortable discussing them with managers. Given that Black women are already underrepresented in senior leadership, menopause can become another barrier to career progression.

5. Culturally Specific Solutions Are Needed

General menopause resources often fail to address the unique needs of Black women. For instance:

- Lifestyle advice may not consider cultural diets or exercise habits.

- Medical advice may overlook differences in how conditions like cardiovascular disease or fibroids (more common in Black women) intersect with menopause.

- Leadership coaching and workplace policies rarely acknowledge the added burden of race and gender on Black women leaders managing menopause while navigating professional spaces.

Conclusion: Why Focus on Black Women Leaders?

Black women in leadership face a double burden — navigating the physical challenges of menopause and the racialised and gendered barriers in professional settings. Without targeted support, many will leave leadership roles prematurely, widening the representation gap.

Focusing on Black women leaders ensures that workplace policies, healthcare interventions, and coaching strategies centre their lived experiences, leading to better retention, career longevity, and overall well-being.

In the context of Black women and menopause, the Superwoman schema refers to the internalised belief that Black women must always be strong, self-sacrificing, and resilient, even at the cost of their own health and well-being. This can lead to delaying menopause care, not seeking support, or feeling pressure to push through symptoms in leadership roles.

Crying can be a surprisingly effective and healthy outlet, especially for menopausal women dealing with the unique emotional and physical changes that menopause brings. While crying might feel uncomfortable, it has several scientifically backed benefits, releasing certain chemicals and hormones that can help with stress, pain, and even improve mood.

Leadership Life Lessons After the Cape Has Gone:

Six key lessons that I have learned about crying.

1. Release of Stress Hormones — (Cortisol)
- Crying, especially when it is emotional crying (as opposed to crying from physical pain or reflex tears, like from cutting onions), releases stress hormones and other toxins. It helps flush out cortisol, a primary stress hormone, from the body, which can help alleviate the physical toll of stress.

- Menopausal women often experience heightened cortisol due to the body's fluctuating hormonal levels. Crying can be a gentle, natural way to counterbalance these surges.

2. Stimulation of Endorphins and Oxytocin
- When you cry, your body produces endorphins and oxytocin, the feel-good and bonding hormones. This chemical release can function as a natural painkiller, lowering the perception of pain and helping to soothe physical and emotional distress.
- This effect can be particularly beneficial for menopausal women experiencing joint pain, headaches, or other discomforts that can accompany menopause.

3. Improved Mood and Emotional Release
- Crying allows a healthy release of pent-up emotions. For women in menopause, it is common to experience mood swings and heightened emotional sensitivity, partly due to hormonal changes.
- Crying can provide a natural outlet for sadness, frustration, or overwhelm, helping to avoid emotional buildup.
- Studies show that crying triggers parasympathetic nervous system activity, which can help induce calm after the release, creating a 'rebound effect' where people feel better than before they cried.

4. Activation of the Parasympathetic Nervous System (PNS)
- The PNS plays a key role in the body's rest-and-digest mode. Crying can help activate this system, bringing the heart rate down, slowing breathing, and relaxing muscles. For menopausal women who may be experiencing anxiety, heart

palpitations, or high blood pressure, this calming effect can provide relief.

5. Encouragement of Social Connection
- Although crying can be a private experience, it often evokes empathy and connection when shared with others. For menopausal women who might be feeling isolated or unsupported in their journey, crying around trusted friends or loved ones can foster a sense of connection and reduce loneliness.

6. Release of Stress-Related Toxins
- Some research suggests that tears carry away excess manganese, a mineral associated with anxiety and irritability. Menopausal women can experience more intense feelings of anxiety due to hormonal fluctuations, so crying may help in maintaining a better emotional balance by reducing excess manganese in the body.

While crying might seem like an indication of vulnerability, it is a powerful self-soothing mechanism that can improve mental and physical well-being. Encouragingly, it is a safe, natural tool for menopausal women to manage stress, pain, and emotional upheaval. It is also a reminder to seek or create supportive environments where letting go of emotions feels safe and understood.

Revisiting Identity

In reflecting on my own experiences, I find that insights from Bell Hooks' *Sisters of the Yam: Black women and Self-Recovery* resonate deeply with me. Hooks dives into the complexities of Black female identity and how we often look toward white culture for validation. This external validation can lead to a fractured sense of self, as we navigate the intersection of racism and sexism. I have felt this acutely, the constant search for acceptance contributing to feelings of inadequacy and imposter syndrome. Despite my accomplishments, I have doubted my abilities and felt like I did not belong. Hooks emphasises the importance of self-recovery and healing, urging us to reclaim our identity and find strength in our cultural heritage.

As a Black British woman who has worn the metaphorical Superwoman cape throughout my career, I have often concealed my vulnerabilities, striving for excellence. This book complements my semi-autobiographical journey, providing a theoretical framework that mirrors my personal experiences. It highlights the pressures we face to conform to external standards, a struggle I know all too well.

I have come to realise that my decision to remove the Superwoman cape and embrace my true self is a powerful act. In revealing and celebrating my vulnerability, I find strength and authenticity. For example, there was a time when I faced a major professional setback. Instead of putting on a brave face and hiding my disappointment, I chose to share my feelings with my colleagues. To my surprise, their support and understanding not only helped me heal but also strengthened our team bond.

Another instance where I found strength in vulnerability was during a public speaking event. I had always maintained a stoic persona but, this time, I decided to share my personal journey and the challenges I have faced as a Black woman. The response was overwhelming — many in the audience felt a deep connection and were inspired by my authenticity.

Brené Brown's work on vulnerability has been instrumental in my journey. She argues that vulnerability is not a weakness, but a source of strength. Embracing vulnerability leads to deeper connections and a more meaningful life.

This combination of personal experience and theoretical insights creates a compelling narrative for my readers. It encourages us, as Black women, to shed the unrealistic expectations of perfection, reclaim our identity, and find strength in our vulnerabilities. My journey is a testament to the power of self-discovery and empowerment, and I hope it inspires others to embark on their own paths of healing and self-recovery.

Reflective Questions for the Black Woman Reader

1. What messages have I internalised about showing emotion, and how have they shaped the way I express or suppress my tears?

2. Where do I feel safest to release my emotions, and how can I create more of those spaces in my personal and professional life?

3. How can I redefine strength for myself in a way that allows vulnerability to coexist with resilience?

Reflective Questions for the Non-Black Coach (Cultural Confidence and Effective Inquiry)

1. How might cultural and racial dynamics influence the way Black women experience and express vulnerability in predominantly white spaces?

2. What assumptions do I hold about emotional expression, and how might these impact the way I support Black women in coaching conversations?

3. How can I create a coaching environment where Black women feel safe enough to share their emotions without fear of judgment or stereotype reinforcement?

Burning My Superwoman Cape: Leadership Lessons Coming Back from a Lifetime of Disrespect

Case Study: Navigating Disrespect in Leadership
Dr Amina Diallo*, a senior healthcare executive, had spent years proving her worth in an organisation where she was one of the few Black women in leadership. She held multiple degrees, had led transformative projects, and was well-respected in her field. Yet, during a high-profile strategy meeting, her expertise was consistently undermined.*

A junior colleague interrupted her mid-sentence to explain a concept she had pioneered. When Amina calmly reasserted her point, the room fell silent, and a senior leader quipped, "Let's not get emotional about this." She recognised the microaggressions immediately — the constant interruptions, the undermining, the subtle policing of her tone. This was not new.

Later that day, Amina reflected on the emotional toll of these interactions. She knew she had choices: confront it directly, document the pattern for future action, or preserve her peace and choose her battles. As a Black woman in leadership, she constantly walked the tightrope between asserting herself and navigating the backlash that often followed.

For much of my life, I have encountered disrespect in its many forms. As a Black woman, the layers of this disrespect have been compounded by race, gender, and often by sheer ignorance. I have been racially abused on the streets while going about my legitimate business. In my younger years, this was a life-or-death matter, requiring an immediate reaction. I felt the weight of needing to defend my dignity, to fight back in a world that seemed intent on stripping me of it.

But now, as I step into my sixth decade on this earth, I have chosen a different path. I no longer react instinctively to every slight, every sneer, or every unkind word. Instead, I respond — often with silence. This is not about passivity or surrender. It is about sovereignty. It is about protecting my energy, my dignity, and my peace. I have come to realise that not every act of disrespect warrants a reaction. My energy is precious, especially as a menopausal woman and wasting it on nonsensical interactions is a cost I am unwilling to pay.

In my earlier years, reacting to disrespect felt like a necessity. It was my way of asserting my humanity in a world that too often denied it. The racial abuse on the streets was visceral and inescapable. It felt like an attack on my very existence, and I met it with the strength and defiance that survival demanded. There were times I needed to confront it head-on because, for a younger me, silence felt like complicity.

But as I have grown older and gained wisdom, I have learned that true power lies in discernment. There is a difference between reacting and responding. Reaction is immediate, emotional, and often draining. Response is deliberate, measured, and rooted in self-awareness. Today, I choose the latter because it aligns with my strategy for maintaining energy and well-being. This is not avoidance; it is mastery.

There are moments, particularly in the workplace, where the dynamics of white privilege and power come into play. In a team meeting, when I have been dismissed or spoken over, the younger version of me would have fought to reclaim the floor. Now, I understand that the most powerful statement I can sometimes make is my refusal to engage in battles that do not serve me. I choose to create my own narrative, to redirect the focus, and to wield my emotional intelligence as a shield.

I have encountered countless microaggressions while shopping, where I have been followed or ignored. In these moments, my silence is not weakness. It is a conscious choice to preserve my dignity. The world expects Black women to carry anger, to respond with fire. By refusing to conform to these expectations, I reclaim my power. My silence speaks volumes; it says, "You will not dictate how I feel or how I use my energy."

Over the years, I have honed my ability to assess situations and decide where to invest my emotions. This has become a cornerstone of my leadership philosophy. Emotional intelligence, insight, and wisdom are tools I use to navigate disrespect. They allow me to remain centred and

focused on what truly matters. I have learned to prioritise my well-being above the fleeting satisfaction of a reaction.

It is not that I am immune to the sting of disrespect. It still hurts. But I have reframed these moments as opportunities to protect my sovereignty. By refusing to engage, I remind myself that my worth is not defined by someone else's inability to see it. My silence is not submission; it is strength.

This approach has also allowed me to find joy amid the challenges. By letting go of the need to react to every instance of disrespect, I have created space for rest, reflection, and growth. I have learned to channel my energy into things that nourish me — relationships, creativity, and the pursuit of justice on my own terms. This is how I maintain my equilibrium, even in a world that often feels unbalanced.

Burning my Superwoman cape has taught me that I do not have to carry the weight of proving my worth to everyone I meet. I do not have to fight every battle. Instead, I choose to live with intention, to respond with purpose, and to protect the dignity that is mine by birthright. This is my power. This is my peace. This is my leadership lesson for the next generation of Black women: your sovereignty is non-negotiable, and your energy is sacred. Choose to use it wisely.

Reflective Questions for the Black Woman Leader:

Reflective Questions for the Non-Black Coach Supporting a Black Client Facing Disrespect:
1. How can I create a psychologically safe space for my client to unpack their experience of disrespect without minimising or overly pathologising their reaction?

2. What culturally competent strategies can I offer to help my client assert their boundaries while safeguarding their emotional wellbeing?

3. How can I challenge my own biases or assumptions to ensure I am fully present and attuned to the racial and gendered nuances of my client's experience?

For non-Black coaches supporting Black women, it's crucial to recognise that experiences of disrespect are not just about workplace dynamics but are often rooted in race, gender, and systemic bias. Coaching Black clients through these challenges requires more than standard leadership advice — it demands cultural awareness, active listening, and an understanding of the emotional and professional toll of racialised experiences. These reflective questions help non-Black coaches examine their approach, ensuring they create a safe, affirming, and empowering coaching space.

Reclaiming My Power: Burning the Superwoman Cape and Embracing My Strength

Burning my Superwoman cape was a radical act of self-reclamation that forced me to confront how I had unknowingly diminished my own power while championing everyone else's. For years, I had believed that wearing the cape — being competent, self-sacrificing, and always available — was a badge of strength. It was a barrier. I made myself small, hiding my voice and my value under the guise of being humble and unassuming. Yet, despite these efforts to remain invisible, I was appointed to leadership roles, not because I worked myself to the bone but because of my personal power — my knowledge, insight, and ability to solve complex challenges. This recognition of my expert power illuminated how much I had ignored my own strengths. Instead of intentionally wielding this power, I had let it be shaped by others' needs, never truly considering how I could use it for my own growth. I also began to understand the value of referent power — the ability to inspire, connect, and build trust. For years, I had underestimated how my authenticity, resilience, and ability to amplify others' voices had earned me respect and influence. These are the same qualities that could have allowed me to lead from a place of wholeness, rather than overwork and self-neglect. Burning the cape was not about abandoning responsibility; it was about redistributing my energy, setting boundaries, and recognising that my power — both personal and relational — could create greater impact when wielded intentionally.

Summary and Reflective Exercise: Reclaiming Power

Power is often seen through the lens of authority, control, or dominance, but for Black women navigating leadership, power can also be deeply personal rooted in resilience, lived experience, and authenticity. French and Raven's framework identifies five bases of power:

- **Legitimate Power** – Authority that comes from a formal position or title.

- **Reward Power** – The ability to give benefits or incentives.

- **Coercive Power** – Influence through fear or punishment.

- **Expert Power** – Power derived from knowledge, skills, or expertise.

- **Referent Power** – Influence built through relationships, respect, and authenticity.

For Black women, expert power and referent power are often under-recognised yet deeply transformative. We may struggle with self-doubt or imposter syndrome, even when our expertise is evident. At the same time, our ability to inspire through our stories, presence, and authenticity – our referent power – can create lasting impact.

Reflections for Black women

- **Recognising Your Expert Power** – Write down one way your knowledge, experience, or skills have positioned you as an expert, even in moments when you doubted yourself. What did others see in you that you struggled to acknowledge?

- **Harnessing Your Referent Power** – Think about how your authenticity, presence, or story has inspired or uplifted others.

How do people respond to your leadership, even when you are not consciously 'leading'?

- **Reclaiming Your Power with Intention** — Take a few minutes to journal: *How can I use my expert and referent power to lead more intentionally — for my own growth, joy, and impact?* End by writing down three actions you will take to celebrate and embody your power more fully.

Before engaging with the reflective questions below, it's important to understand that power — particularly for Black women — often exists in spaces of tension: between expertise and doubt, leadership and invisibility, resilience and exhaustion. By reflecting on power in a way that centres personal agency and authenticity, Black women can reclaim their leadership with intention. For non-Black coaches, these questions serve as an entry point into deeper awareness and more effective, affirming coaching.

Guidance for Non-Black Coaches

Understanding how power operates differently for Black women in leadership is critical for effective coaching. Consider these questions:

- **How do I acknowledge and validate the expert and referent power of Black women, especially when they downplay their own achievements?**
  Black women often face systemic biases that make their expertise less visible or validated. Your role as a coach includes helping them own their brilliance without apology.

- **How do I recognise and challenge my own assumptions about power and leadership?**
  Traditional models of power often centre dominant cultural norms. Consider whether your coaching approach assumes

power must look a certain way and how you can expand that understanding.

- **How can I create a coaching space that affirms Black women's unique experiences of power, visibility, and resilience?**
Psychological safety matters. Acknowledge the emotional labour and systemic challenges Black women navigate and create space for them to express their experiences without judgment.

Transforming Anger into Liberation

Releasing anger accumulated from years of experiencing racism can be a profound and transformative journey for Black women. Audre Lorde famously spoke about the dual nature of anger, recognising it not just as a powerful emotion but also as a form of grief – a mourning of the injustices faced. She argued that anger, when harnessed and expressed creatively, can become a source of strength, clarity, and even healing.

I have spent over thirty years leading in the social world of EDI, was in many corporate spaces and have never ceased to be curious as an EDI specialist. My work has demanded an immense level of affective labour, requiring me to engage deeply with diverse communities, often in volatile or highly distressed circumstances. I have faced individuals and groups expressing frustration, fear, or anger, sometimes directed at me simply because I represent a system they feel has failed them. Despite this, the role requires me to consistently use emotional intelligence – staying open, empathetic, and composed – while enabling understanding and fostering collaboration. Over the years, the cumulative toll of navigating such intense emotional landscapes has coincided with a personal transition: the depletion of hormones during menopause has made historical coping strategies increasingly ineffective. The proverbial Superwoman cape, once a symbol of my ability to push through challenges with resilience, no longer shields me from feelings of vulnerability or projects an image of invincibility. This stage of life has brought a need for recalibration — moving into different networks and communities that provide support and understanding. It is a humbling but necessary shift, acknowledging that the emotional labour required in EDI work, paired with the changes menopause brings, makes self-preservation and the pursuit of environments that nurture rather than drain me more critical than ever.

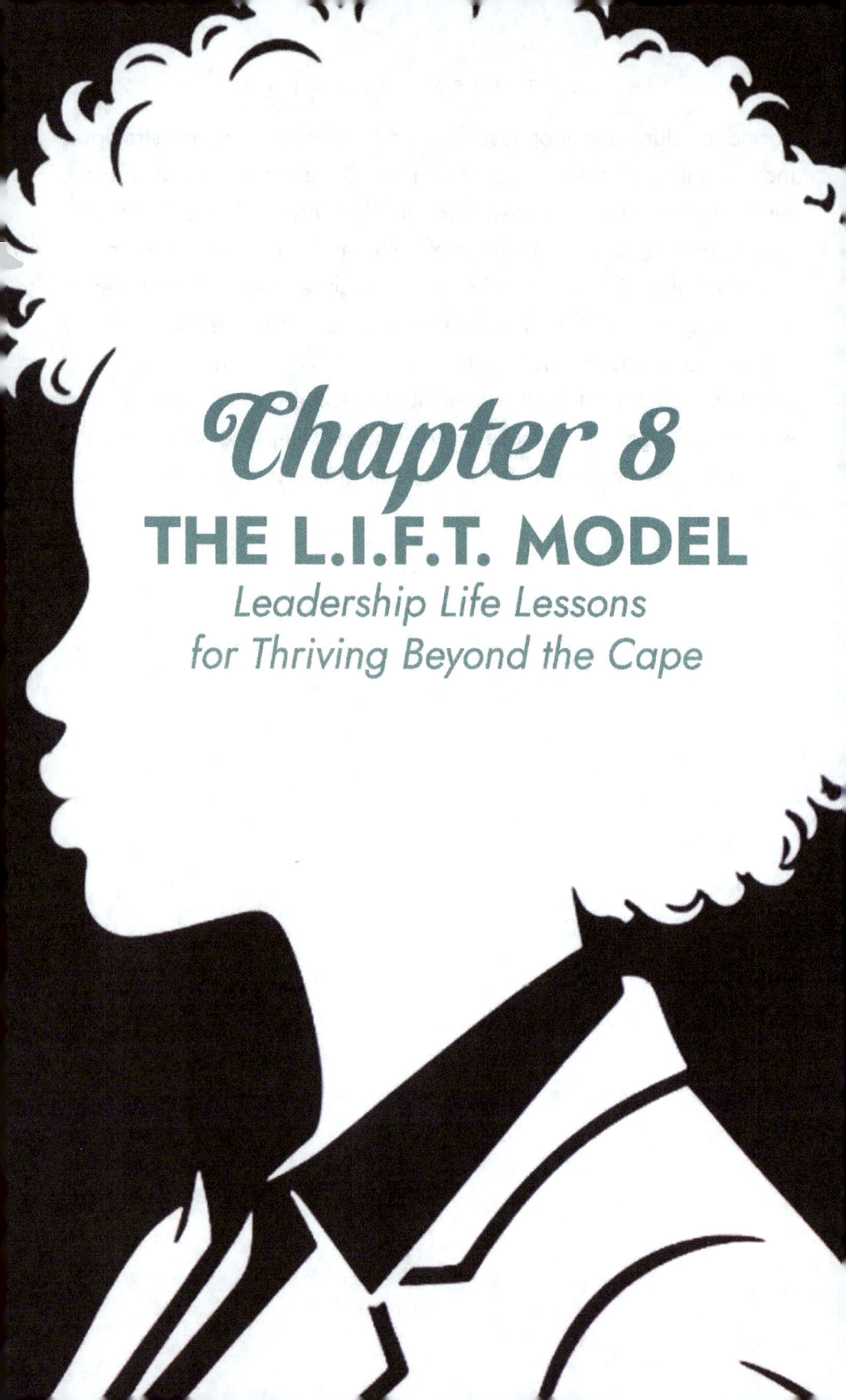
Chapter 8
THE L.I.F.T. MODEL
Leadership Life Lessons for Thriving Beyond the Cape

Introduction to the Chapter

Why the L.I.F.T. Model?

Throughout this book, I have shared my journey of shedding the 'Superwoman cape' — the weight of expectations, the struggle with imposter syndrome, and the challenges of navigating leadership as a Black woman. But once the cape is gone, what comes next? How do we lead with authenticity, reclaim our identity, and build a fulfilling and sustainable career and life?

This is where the L.I.F.T. Model comes in. It is a framework for leadership renewal, a guide to help you lead without self-sacrifice, embrace your identity, find joy beyond professional success, and build a strong support network.

Too often, women — especially women of colour — are expected to do it all: lead, nurture, fight for recognition, and still hold everything together. But leadership does not have to come at the cost of well-being. The L.I.F.T. Model provides a structured approach to leading with confidence, without burnout.

What is the L.I.F.T. Model?

L.I.F.T. stands for:

- **L**eadership — Redefining leadership as authenticity, impact, and self-trust.

- **I**dentity — Embracing your full self, free from external expectations and imposter syndrome.

- **F**ulfilment — Prioritising well-being, rest, and joy over toxic productivity.

- Togetherness — Building networks, mentorship, and collective resilience.

The L.I.F.T. Model is designed to help you:

✓ Step into leadership with clarity and confidence

✓ Overcome imposter syndrome and self-doubt

✓ Create balance between success and personal fulfilment

✓ Build meaningful connections that sustain your growth

How to Use the L.I.F.T. Model

This chapter will break down each element of the model, sharing real-life examples, leadership lessons, and practical exercises. By the end, you will have a personalised strategy for leading in a way that aligns with who you truly are — without the exhaustion of performing for others.

But before we dive into the model, let's start with a case study — a real-life example of how leadership, identity, fulfilment, and togetherness shape our journeys.

Chapter 9
CASE STUDIES

Breaking Free from the Superwoman cape

Meet Ava — A High-Achieving Leader Battling Burnout

Ava had always been the go-to person in her organisation. A senior leader in the public sector, she was known for her sharp mind, her ability to manage it all, and her unwavering commitment to diversity and inclusion. She was a mentor, a leader, and often, the only Black woman in the room.

But behind the scenes, Ava was struggling.

She worked longer hours than her colleagues, feeling the need to prove herself constantly. She sat in meetings where her ideas were overlooked, only to be repeated by someone else moments later. She mentored others but had no mentor herself. She felt exhausted, questioning if she truly belonged at the table.

Her personal life was suffering — she barely made time for her own well-being, her stress levels were affecting her health, and she felt disconnected from the joy she once had in her career. She knew something had to change.

A Turning Point

Ava attended a leadership retreat where she was introduced to the L.I.F.T. Model. For the first time, she realised leadership was not about doing more but about leading differently.

- ✓ **She redefined leadership** by setting boundaries and recognising that her worth wasn't tied to overworking.
- ✓ **She embraced her identity**, no longer shrinking herself in spaces that didn't fully value her.

- ✓ **She prioritised fulfilment**, setting aside time for joy and self-care.

- ✓ **She leaned into togetherness**, seeking mentorship and building a support system.

Within months, Ava felt lighter, more in control, and more fulfilled in her role. She wasn't just surviving — she was thriving.

Reflections

Can you see yourself in Ava's story? Have you ever felt the pressure to overperform, prove yourself, or neglect your own well-being?

As you read this chapter, think about your own leadership journey. Where do you need L.I.F.T. the most? Let's explore how this model can help you lead with purpose, without the burnout.

Chapter 10
TIPS AND TOOLS

Leadership Lessons After the Cape Has Gone:

Here are six practical tools I have used over the years as creative outlets to help channel my anger and grief into pathways which have enabled and nurtured my well-being.

Three Personal Leadership Life Lessons and Supportive Strategies

1. Lesson: Vulnerability Is a Strength, Not a Weakness

2. Lesson: Prioritising Rest and Boundaries is Essential

Supporting Strategies:

- **Establish Clear Boundaries:** Set firm work-life boundaries to prevent burnout, such as defining non-negotiable rest periods or limiting after-hours engagement.

- **Adopt a Rest Ethic:** Integrate restorative practices, like mindfulness, yoga, or leisure activities, as essential parts of your routine rather than optional luxuries.

- **Delegate Effectively:** Identify tasks that can be shared with or transferred to others, empowering colleagues while reducing your load.

3. Lesson: Personal Growth Requires Adaptation Useful Reflection Tools

Supportive and Enabling Strategies:

- **Expand Networks:** Actively seek out new professional and social communities that align with your current needs and offer mutual learning opportunities.

- **Redefine Success:** Shift focus from the Superwoman ideal to realistic, sustainable goals that balance ambition with well-being.

Invest in Continuous Learning: Pursue resources or training to develop new coping mechanisms tailored to this stage of life, such as workshops on managing menopause and emotional resilience.

1. Journaling and Storytelling

The Practice: Dedicate time each day or week to write freely about your experiences, feelings, and frustrations. Let your anger spill onto the pages without censoring yourself. This can be done through traditional journaling or digital platforms.

Why It Works: Writing serves as a safe container to unload the weight of unspoken grievances. It is a form of self-validation and reclaiming your narrative. By turning anger into written words, you can begin to understand its layers, including the grief beneath it, and transform pain into stories of resilience.

Creative Twist: Consider writing poetry, short stories, or even anonymous blog posts. Turning raw anger into art can provide a sense of empowerment and control over your narrative.

2. Anger Release Rituals

Transforming Anger into Liberation. Embracing anger as both a response to injustice and as a form of grief can be revolutionary. By engaging in creative practices, Black women can transform their anger into sources of strength, healing, and community. These tools not only honour the complexity of their emotions but also create new spaces for joy, rest, and radical self-care.

The Practice: Develop personal rituals that allow you to physically release anger. This could involve activities like:

Screaming into a pillow: A cathartic release when words are not enough.

Smashing objects: Using items like old plates or clay pots that you can safely break to symbolise breaking free from oppressive experiences.

Burning Letters: Write letters to those who have wronged you or to racism itself, expressing all your suppressed anger, then burn them safely as a symbolic release.

Why It Works: These rituals tap into the physicality of anger, giving your body a chance to release pent-up tension. The act of destroying something or witnessing the transformation of fire can be incredibly liberating and symbolises letting go.

3. Movement and Dance

The Practice: Engage in movement that allows you to express rage, sorrow, and joy. Dance styles like Afrobeats, dancehall, or even freestyle can help you tap into the primal energy of anger and transform it into power I undertake somatic yoga.

Why It Works: Movement is a way to reclaim agency over your body, especially when society has tried to police or devalue it. Dancing can help transmute anger into a celebration of your physical and spiritual self, channelling grief into something life-affirming.

Creative Twist: Create a playlist of songs that reflect your journey – from rage to release to reclamation – and let your body move through those emotional stages.

4. Art Therapy: Painting, Drawing, and Collage

The Practice: Use art as a non-verbal way of expressing anger. Abstract painting, for example, allows you to translate intense emotions onto canvas without the need for words. Alternatively, collaging can be a way to visualise breaking down oppressive structures and reassembling them in your own image.

Why It Works: Art provides a space to externalise your feelings, turning them into something tangible. This process can be deeply healing, as it allows you to see your emotions reflected outside of yourself, providing a new perspective and a sense of release.

Creative Twist: Create a series of pieces titled The Anatomy of My Anger or Grief Unveiled that visually depict your journey through rage, sorrow, and healing.

5. Vocal Expression: Singing, Chanting, and Spoken Word

The Practice: Use your voice to release what has been buried inside. This can be through singing songs that resonate with your experiences, chanting affirmations, or performing spoken word poetry that confronts racial trauma and celebrates your resilience.

Why It Works: The vibration of your own voice is powerful in releasing trapped emotions. It is a reclamation of your right to be heard. Audre Lorde used poetry as a weapon, a tool for survival, and a method of reclaiming space.

Creative Twist: Record yourself performing your pieces and consider sharing them with a trusted community or online space to inspire others.

6. Organic-Based Practices

The Practice: Engage in rituals that connect you with nature to ground and release your anger. Consider practices such as:

Forest Bathing: Spending intentional time in nature to reconnect with the earth and release heavy emotions.

Creating Herbal Blends: Using herbs like lavender, chamomile, to create teas, bath soaks, or incense blends that calm the nervous system and release tension.

Why It Works: Nature has a way of absorbing and neutralising energy. By channelling your anger into nature-based practices, you align with the natural cycle of release and renewal, finding comfort in ancestral connections to the earth.

Creative Twist: Grow a resilience garden with plants that symbolise strength and healing. Each time you tend to your garden, you are not just nurturing the plants but also your own spirit.

7. Community Healing Circles

The Practice: Gather with other Black women to create a safe space for sharing stories, experiences, and collective grief. Use practices like guided meditation, sound baths, or collective chanting to release emotions together.

Why It Works: There is profound healing in being witnessed and supported by those who understand your struggles. A collective release amplifies the power of individual healing, turning isolation into solidarity.

Creative Twist: Start a monthly Grief and Anger Circle where women can come together to creatively release anger through shared activities like painting, writing, or even collective dance.

8. Creative Activism

The Practice: Channel your anger into activism by creating something that brings about social change. This could be through art installations, writing letters to institutions, starting a podcast, or organizing community events.

Why It Works: Transforming anger into action is a way to take back power. It shifts the narrative from victimhood to agency, turning the personal into the political and giving purpose to the pain.

Creative Twist: Start a magazine or blog that highlights the experiences of Black women navigating anger and grief, using it as a platform to inspire others and create a ripple effect of healing.

As I wrote *Rest, Rise, Reclaim*, I kept returning to two internalised roles that have shaped — and sometimes stifled — my leadership journey: the Black Superwoman syndrome and imposter syndrome.

These tools are designed to help you gently explore and challenge these roles, understanding not just what you're doing or feeling, but also why — and most importantly, how you can begin to reclaim your own story.

They are simple, accessible self-coaching frameworks that you can return to regularly. Whether you are reading this for personal reflection, group dialogue, or using them as a coach to support others, these grids are invitations — not judgements. Use them to pause, reframe, and take back your power.

Instructions for Use (Place as Guidance Text Above the Table):
- In the **WHAT** column, name the thought, behaviour, or feeling linked to imposter syndrome.

- In the **WHY** column, reflect on where this may come from — early experiences, workplace culture, or internalised messages.

- In the **HOW** column, write one small step you can take to reclaim your confidence or reframe the belief.

A Note to Coaches and System Leaders:

These tools can be adapted for coaching sessions, group workshops, or leadership retreats. Invite your clients to reflect, write freely, and revisit these grids over time. They are not fixed worksheets — they are portals to reclaiming voice, truth, and choice.

Shedding the Cape and Reclaiming Self – Reflective Coaching Tools

As I wrote *Rest, Rise, Reclaim*, I kept returning to two internalised roles that have shaped — and sometimes stifled — my leadership journey, the *Black Superwoman* Syndrome and imposter Syndrome. These tools are designed to help you gently explore and challenge these roles, understanding not just what you're doing or feeling, but also *why* — and most importantly, *how* you can begin to reclaim you own story.

1: The Black Superwoman Syndrome Grid – „Unpacking the Cape"

WHAT am I doing or feeling? (The Cape in action)	WHY do I feel I must do this? (Cultural/ internal drivers)	HOW will I begin to shift this?
I never show vulnerability in the workplace.	I was raised to believe showing emotion is weakness	I will allow myself to feel and hame m emotions in safe
I carry the emotional weight of my family	I've always been "the strong one"	I will set healthy boundarize and prioritize rest
I overfunction in relationships	I fear being seen as needy or dependent	I will ask for support and delegate when needed

2: The Imposter Syndrome Grid – „Naming the Inner Doubt"

WHAT am I feeling or doing?	WHY am I feeling or doing this?	HOW can I begin to shift this
I minimize my success in meetings	I worry others think I don't deserve to be here	I'll start documenting my wins and share one each week with a pear or coach
I prepare obsessevly to avold mistakes.	I believe I must be twice as good to be seen as competent	I'll reflect on what "good enough" looks like in healthy terms

Chapter 11
FINAL THOUGHTS
After the Cape Is Burnt:
Leadership Life Lessons

BEVERLEY A. POWELL

Burning My Superwoman Cape: Leadership Life Lessons After the Cape Has Gone

Reflecting on my leadership journey, I now see how much the world of work has transformed from the days when holding a local job for life was the ultimate aspiration. Back then, work was transactional clock in, clock out, and get paid for a week's honest labour, in the hand, by way of a wage packet. Today, jobs are rarely for life. People relocate from their families for wider career opportunities, pursue portfolio careers, and thrive in a global economy fuelled by instant connectivity. This is vastly different from the days of global connectivity and excitement via receipt of an airmail stamp or a telegram. Technology and societal shifts have redefined not only how we work but also how we live and the different ways one can be part of global communities.

Education, once a straight road to a fixed career, has become a winding, unpredictable path. My own leadership and academic journey reflect this; it is the detours, not just the destinations, which have shaped me. Moving from local grassroots projects to regional, national, and global leadership roles representing organisations has taught me that adaptability and lifelong learning are key. At the same time, workplaces have evolved to reflect a broader understanding of the human experience. Topics such as the menopause, once shrouded in silence, are now openly discussed, and formalised through organisational policies fostering environments where women finally feel seen, heard, valued, and supported. Parental leave which once felt like a privilege, is now increasingly recognised as a right, demonstrating a commitment to diversity, equity, and work–life balance in the workplace.

The best organisations today are not just transactional; they lead with values of EDI. They recognise that leadership and innovation thrive on diversity of thought, backgrounds, and experiences. Entrepreneurs, too, reflect this shift, bringing bold, inclusive ideas to the table.

If I have learned anything, it is this: success in today's world demands not only courage but compassion for self and others and embracing a non-linear path. Seek organisations that value the whole person and engage with diverse voices and perspectives. Whether working for someone else or building your own enterprise, grab life by the scruff of its neck. Leadership is not about wearing a cape — it is about letting it go and leading with authenticity and purpose.

Leadership Life Lessons: The Power of Self-Validation and Honouring My Innate Wisdom

For much of my 40-plus-year career, I sought validation from external sources — colleagues, managers, institutions, and even the broader societal gaze that often dictated whose contributions were acknowledged and whose were ignored. I believed that if I worked twice as hard, delivered excellence, and showed unwavering commitment, my worth would be recognised. But the reality of navigating leadership as a Black woman meant that recognition was often inconsistent, conditional, or absent altogether.

I have led in spaces where I was the only one who looked like me, where my presence was questioned, and where my expertise was doubted despite my qualifications and achievements. I have given my all to organisations that benefited from my intellect, strategic thinking, and leadership but were slow to acknowledge my value. For years, I internalised the idea that my worth was tied to external approval. That changed when I realised that waiting for validation from systems not designed to see me was a losing battle.

What I failed to do — what I was conditioned to ignore — was lean into the deep, ancestral wisdom already within me; the wisdom passed down from generations of strong Black women before me. They were women who survived, thrived, and built legacies without waiting for permission or recognition. Instead, I spent years looking outward for affirmation, when all along, my own lived experience – my struggles, victories, intuition – was a source of wisdom I could have trusted.

For too long, I ignored the voice inside me that whispered, *you know what to do*. I dismissed my instincts in favour of external validation. I silenced the lessons that came from being a soul having a human experience in a heterosexual, Black, cis woman's body – a body and existence shaped by struggle and resilience, by systemic barriers and ancestral power. It took me decades to realise the systems I was trying to impress were never meant to hold space for my truth. So why was I still trying to fit into them?

How I Discovered Self-Validation

There was no singular moment when self-validation clicked for me; instead, it was a gradual awakening, shaped by years of experiences, disappointments, and small victories. I remember a time when I put everything into a project – long hours, strategic thinking, delivering beyond expectations – only for my contribution to be overlooked in the final acknowledgements. I felt invisible. That moment stung, but it also sparked something in me: a quiet rebellion against the need for external approval.

I asked myself: *if no one claps, does that make my work any less impactful?* The answer was a resounding *no*.

I started redefining success on my own terms. I stopped waiting for others to recognise my value and began recognising it for myself. I gave myself permission to be proud of what I had accomplished, whether anyone else acknowledged it or not. It was liberating.

But even deeper than that, I began tuning in to the wisdom I had once ignored. I started listening to the quiet knowing within me — the kind that told me when to walk away from spaces that didn't serve me, when to stop overexplaining myself, and when to trust my lived experience as truth.

What Self-Validation Is (and What It Is Not)

Self-validation is the ability to recognise and affirm your own worth, regardless of external opinions. It means trusting your experiences, acknowledging your achievements, and accepting that you are enough. It is a leadership skill, a survival mechanism, and an act of self-preservation.

Self-validation is *not* arrogance, nor is it about disregarding feedback or input from others. Instead, it is about knowing that your value does not decrease because someone else fails to see it.

How Self-Validation Changed Me

Discovering self-validation changed how I viewed myself and my leadership. I no longer needed permission to take up space, to rest, or to celebrate myself. It shifted my inner dialogue — where once I second-guessed myself, I now remind myself: I am *here because I deserve to be*.

It also brought me peace. No longer chasing approval meant I could focus my energy on what truly mattered: impact, growth, and joy. I learned to acknowledge my wins, no matter how small. I found joy in my own recognition, rather than waiting for someone else's. And most importantly, I realised the most powerful validation I could ever receive was my own.

Key Leadership Life Lessons on Self-Validation

- **You set the standard for your own worth.**
  No one else can dictate how valuable you are. If you don't believe in your own capabilities, it's easy for others to diminish them.

- **Silence the inner critic.**
  The loudest voice you hear should be your own — and it should be one of encouragement, not self-doubt. Reframe negative self-talk and remind yourself of your accomplishments.

- **Seek feedback, but don't depend on it.**
  Constructive feedback is essential for growth, but it should never be the sole determinant of your self-worth. Accept feedback, but remember that your value exists regardless of external opinions.

- **Celebrate yourself unapologetically.**
  I no longer wait for others to acknowledge my achievements. I recognise my own progress, whether that's through journaling, treating myself, or simply taking a moment to say, "I did that."

- **Rest is a form of validation.**
  Resting is an act of self-acknowledgment. It says, "I have done enough. I am enough." The Superwoman cape had me believing that constant work was the only measure of worth. Now, I validate myself through balance, boundaries, and intentional rest.

> - **Your impact is bigger than immediate recognition.** Some of the greatest work we do won't receive applause in the moment. But true leadership isn't about instant validation — it's about lasting impact. My legacy is built not on who applauded me, but on the lives I've influenced, the barriers I've broken, and the wisdom I've passed on.

Self-Reflection: Embracing Your Own Validation

As you reach this point in the book, I encourage you to reflect on your own journey with self-validation. Take some time to respond to the following four questions:

Self-validation is a leadership skill as much as a personal one. It is the foundation of resilience, confidence, and joy. My leadership journey has taught me that when you validate yourself, you no longer need permission to shine. You shine because you know your light is undeniable.

Where do you currently seek validation the most?
From colleagues, leaders, social media, family, or within yourself?

How do you talk to yourself about your achievements?
Do you acknowledge them fully, or downplay them?

What is one moment in your career where you validated yourself instead of waiting for others to do it?
How did that feel?

What small action can you take today to practice self-validation?
Writing a note to yourself, celebrating a recent success, or reminding yourself of your unique brilliance?

So, as I close this book, I invite you to step into your own power. Validate yourself. Celebrate yourself. And never let anyone — including yourself — doubt your worth. Your ancestors, your life experiences, and your wisdom already confirm it.

Reclaiming My Black Joy

- Stepping out from under the Superwoman cape has meant embracing and expressing my Black joy unapologetically, rediscovering laughter and banter as acts of liberation. Black joy is a radiant celebration of our shared humanity, expressed through the rhythms of our music, the richness of our food, the vibrancy of our dance, and the soul-deep connection in our storytelling and patois. It is joy rooted in culture, resistance, and a profound sense of community — a joy that feels effortless and restorative when shared in the comfort of familial and cultural surroundings. However, there is often a subtle fear of sharing this joy too freely around white people, born from the legacy of being surveyed and misunderstood — a hesitance that our unguarded joy might be misinterpreted as being frivolous, lazy, or simply threatening.

Chapter 12
"SELF-CARE IS NOT SELF-INDULGENCE, IT IS SELF-PRESERVATION."
AUDRE LORDE

Resilience In the Rubble

In a time of global uncertainty and personal turmoil, I found myself providing strategic leadership on the frontline while managing a crisis that disproportionately devastated Black and brown communities. The pandemic exposed the deep fractures of inequity within systems designed to provide care, but not necessarily care, equitably. As death rates among people who looked like me soared, I faced the complexity of guiding others through fear, anxiety, and grief while wrestling with my own. This chapter is a reflection on leading through a global nightmare when every call was a reminder of personal loss, and every silence brought the crushing weight of loneliness. Yet, amid the chaos, I learned lessons about survival, cultural competency, and the unyielding spirit of resilience channelled through my ancestry.

Resilience has never been accidental. It is the sum of habits, routines, and choices honed over decades — a foundation I leaned on when everything else seemed to crumble. For over forty years I have found solace and kindred spirits in the membership of a gym, a space where the world's demands paused, and I could focus on my own strength, both inner and outer. When the pandemic shut those doors, I adapted. I ordered gym equipment and built an in-house routine that became a lifeline. Movement grounded me, offering a sense of normalcy amid chaos.

Movement became my daily anchor. Short walks around the block during lunch breaks or between meetings provided a chance to clear my head and reconnect with the world outside. These moments, however brief, reminded me that even in chaos, there was still breath, still life.

During this time, I also discovered the transformative power of yoga and meditation. What began as tentative morning stretches to ease the tension in my body quickly evolved into a daily practice of mindfulness. Yoga taught me to listen to my body, while meditation gave me space to quiet the endless noise in my mind. Journaling became another lifeline, a safe place to pour out my fears, frustrations, and reflections. On paper, I found clarity, processing emotions that were otherwise too heavy to carry.

Nutrition also became an area of focus and transformation. While I had always valued balanced eating, this period led me to strip back certain foods and align my meals with what I later understood to be a menopause-focused diet. I will explore this in more detail in a later chapter. For now, I learned the importance of nourishing my body in ways that honoured its changing needs. They were small, intentional choices that worked for me.

Eating well became another pillar of resilience. As the world spiralled, I clung to the basics — balanced meals, hydration, and moments to nourish my body, even when my spirit felt depleted. I carved out time to step outside, walking around the block during lunch breaks or between relentless meetings. Those short bursts of fresh air reminded me that the world, though fractured, still had moments of beauty.

In the quiet hours, I turned my focus to understanding the storm we were in. I studied regional, national, and global mortality data, dissecting statistics through the lens of ethnicity and age. Clinical experts generously shared insights, shedding light on the structural and biological reasons behind the disproportionate loss of Black and brown lives. This knowledge, though devastating, empowered me to advocate more effectively. It became a tool not just for my work but for making sense of the chaos that surrounded me.

Resilience was not about ignoring the pain or pretending it did not exist. It was about finding strength in the familiar and using knowledge as a weapon against despair. These practices, ingrained over decades, did not just sustain me — they allowed me to continue leading through the global shitstorm which impacted everyone.

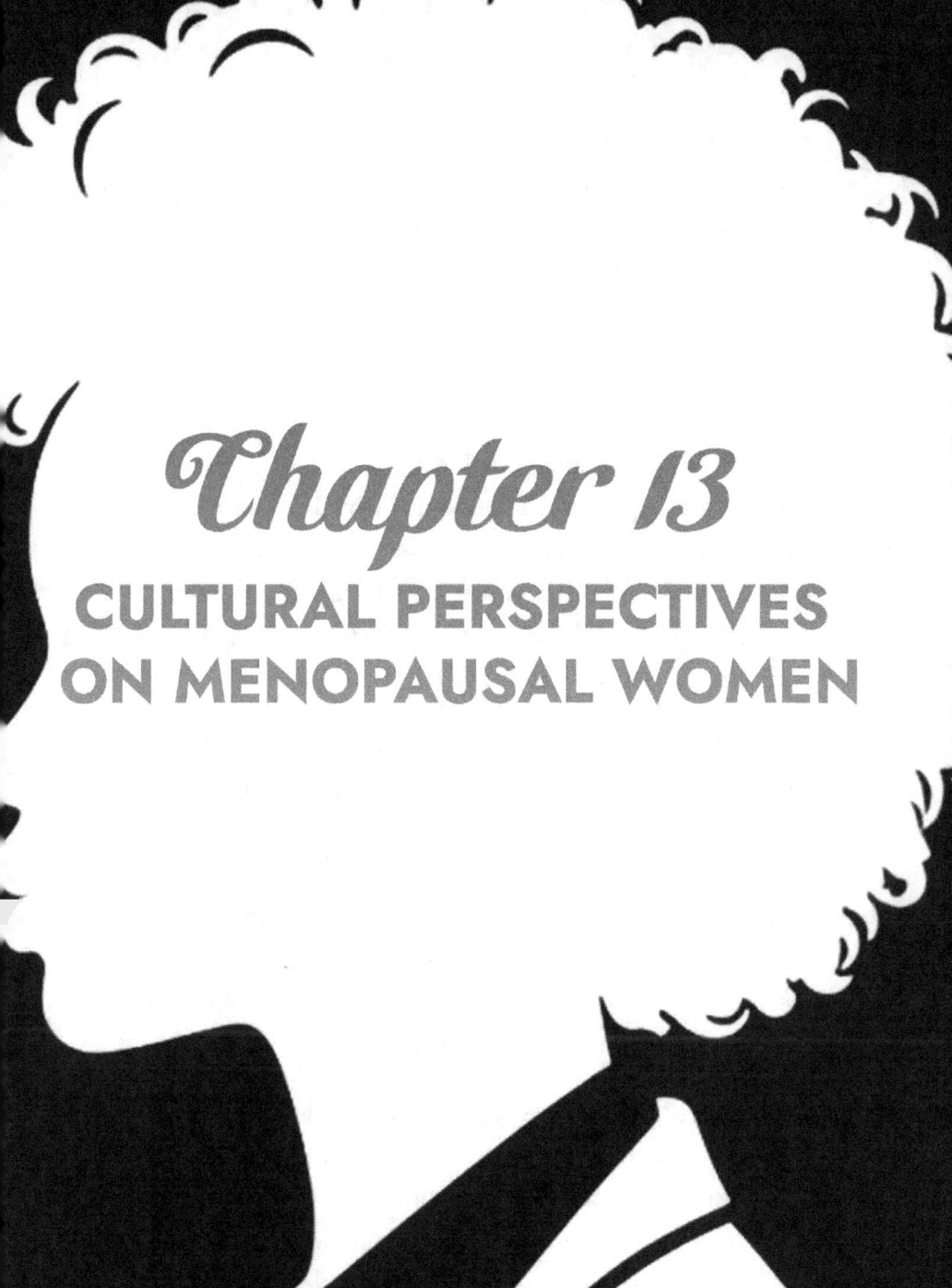

Chapter 13
CULTURAL PERSPECTIVES ON MENOPAUSAL WOMEN

This theme emphasises a holistic journey through retirement, highlighting the transition from years of demanding work to embracing rest, healing, and a deeper exploration of identity. It reflects the richness of this life stage while honouring the unique experiences of Black women.

The views on menopausal women vary significantly across distinct cultures. In Chinese culture, older women hold significant roles, and their wisdom and experience are highly valued. These women are often revered and respected as they enter what are referred to as the 'golden years', a term that celebrates the transition into menopause. This period symbolises a time where women are recognised for their wisdom, maturity, and fulfilment, and where their life experiences and contributions to society are celebrated.

In India and Japan, older women are respected for their wisdom and experience within the family and community. Indigenous cultures around the world offer similar reverence to post-menopausal women. In contrast, many Western cultures place less emphasis on revering older women and, instead, societal pressure tends to focus on maintaining youthfulness through a Western lens of beauty. This difference in perspective highlights the diversity of cultural attitudes towards ageing and the role of women in society.

In the UK, the experience of menopause and post-menopausal women is often accompanied by a sense of not being seen or valued by society. Through my work and insights as a licensed menopause champion, I have observed how societal standards of beauty, which emphasise youthfulness and certain physical attributes, do not celebrate British or European menopausal women. This lack of recognition is further compounded for Black women, who face the additional challenges of racial biases and stereotypes. The intersection of race and age can make the experience of menopause even more isolating, as the unique needs and contributions of Black post-menopausal women often go unnoticed.

Remaining Grounded Amid Chaos

Among the global, national, and local chaos that life can throw at us, I always try to find ways to remain grounded. This practice is ongoing and has enabled me to improve my performance as a transformational leadership coach, sharpen my mind, and work to bring my best self in service of others.

As a Black woman, I have been brave enough to show my humanity and in the past, in cultivated psychologically safe spaces, I have shed my own tears over the notion of 'worthiness'. Living in a Black body, it is not always safe to show my humanity due to potential risks to my safety, career, and life itself. The suppressed trauma is real. What I have learned and appreciated more during this time of my life is that my emotions are sacred and very real. It is part of my humanity to be cherished.

Discovering Joy, Laughter, Vulnerability, and Creativity

Throughout my journey, I have also discovered the immense joy and laughter that come from allowing myself to be vulnerable. Embracing vulnerability has been a powerful tool in connecting with others and finding my own inner strength. By letting down my guard, I have been able to experience genuine happiness and creativity. This newfound openness has allowed me to explore my creative side, whether through writing, art, or simply finding joy in everyday moments.

I stumbled upon an interview with the fabulous Black American Viola Davies this week and captured some of her words for my personal and open blog. It resonated with me deeply. She said:

"No shade on any Black woman who can hold things down. I own my personal power, and I have connected with my humanity by dropping back into the body. Worthy..." **Viola Davies**

If you are embracing the Golden Age of retirement or seeking practical tips and tools, I have set out five reflective questions and five practical tips for you:

Personal Growth and Identity

How have my experiences shaped who I am today?

In what ways can I honour and celebrate my heritage and identity as a Black woman during this stage of my life?

What aspects of my journey bring me the most pride and joy?

Health and Well-being

How can I prioritise my physical, emotional, and mental health as I transition into this new phase?

What are some self-care practices that bring me peace and fulfilment?

How can I create a balanced lifestyle that nurtures my well-being?

Legacy and Contribution

What legacy do I want to leave behind for future generations?

In what ways can I continue to make meaningful contributions to my community and society?

How can I mentor and support younger Black women on their journeys?

Joy and Creativity

What activities bring me joy and allow me to express my creativity?

How can I incorporate more laughter and playfulness into my daily life?

In what ways can I allow myself to be more vulnerable and open to new experiences?

Navigating Challenges

How can I navigate societal pressures and beauty standards that may not reflect my true self?

What support systems do I have in place to help me through challenging times?

How can I advocate for myself and other Black women in similar situations?

Five Practical Leadership Tips

1. **Embrace Self-Care**
    - Prioritise regular check-ups and health screenings.
    - Practice mindfulness and meditation to maintain mental clarity and reduce stress.
    - Engage in physical activities that you enjoy, such as yoga, dancing, or walking.

2. **Nurture Your Creativity**
    - Explore creative outlets like writing, painting, or crafting.
    - Join clubs or groups that share your interests to foster a sense of community.

- Dedicate time each week to engage in activities that inspire and energise you.

3. **Build Support Networks**

    - Connect with other Black women who are navigating similar life stages.
    - Participate in local or online support groups focused on menopause and ageing.
    - Seek out mentors or become a mentor to share experiences and wisdom.

4. **Celebrate Your Identity**

    - Learn more about your cultural heritage and share it with others.
    - Attend events and gatherings that celebrate Black culture and history.
    - Use your voice to advocate for issues that matter to you and your community.

5. **Stay Informed and Empowered**

    - Keep up to date with information on health, wellness, and ageing.
    - Educate yourself about the changes your body may go through during menopause.
    - Take advantage of resources and programmes designed to support women in their golden years.

Over the years I have learned that Black women are often subjected to the 'strong Black woman' or 'Superwoman' trope, which glorifies resilience but simultaneously demands that they be self-sacrificing, impervious to pain, and endlessly capable. This cultural expectation pushes Black women to overextend themselves, whether in the workplace, family life, or community roles, often at the expense of their own well-being.

This trope not only leads to burnout but also discourages Black women from seeking help or rest, as vulnerability is often seen as a luxury they cannot afford. The pressure to be the 'pillar of strength' can prevent Black women from acknowledging their own needs, contributing to mental health issues like anxiety, depression, and high-functioning stress. This societal demand for strength erases the right to rest and recuperation, turning self-care into a radical act of resistance.

Menopause, Ageing and the Superwoman

The experience of menopause for Black women is shaped by biological and social factors. Studies show that Black women tend to experience menopause earlier than their white counterparts and report more severe symptoms, including hot flashes, sleep disturbances, and joint pain. However, the intersection of race and gender means their symptoms are often dismissed or minimised by healthcare providers, who may not take their complaints as seriously.

Also, menopause intersects with the ongoing pressures of being the Superwoman. During this life stage, many Black women are navigating peak career responsibilities, caring for ageing parents, and supporting children or grandchildren, all while managing the physiological changes of menopause. The lack of tailored healthcare support, coupled with societal expectations to be endlessly resilient, exacerbates feelings of isolation and exhaustion.

Mental Health and Racial Trauma

The cumulative impact of navigating systemic racism, sexism, and ageism takes a toll on Black women's mental health. They often face barriers to accessing mental health services due to stigma, financial constraints, and the lack of culturally sensitive care. Even when they do seek help, they may encounter therapists who are ill-equipped to understand the nuances of their lived experiences, leading to misdiagnosis or inadequate support.

The concept of racial battle fatigue describes the psychological weariness that comes from constant exposure to racial microaggressions, discrimination, and systemic inequities. For Black women, this fatigue is compounded by the expectation to maintain composure and strength, often feeling the pressure to represent their entire race in white spaces.

The Right to Reclaim My Joy

In the face of these intersecting oppressions, reclaiming rest is not just a personal act but a political one for Black women. The notion that they deserve rest, joy, and ease challenges the dehumanising stereotypes that have historically been imposed upon them. Movements like the Nap Ministry, founded by Tricia Hersey, emphasise that rest is a form of resistance against capitalism and white supremacy, which have long exploited Black bodies for labour.

Reparation, therefore, must include not only economic and social justice but also a right to rest and cultural shifts that honour the well-being of Black women. It involves creating spaces where Black women can heal from the trauma of their intersecting oppressions, reclaim their narratives, and thrive beyond mere survival.

Arriving at this stage of my life, I have been reminded by several Black women activists of the importance of rest. Audre Lorde reminded us that: "Caring for myself is not self-indulgence, it is self-preservation, and that is an act of political warfare." For Black women, rest is more than a physical act — it is a radical reclaiming of our humanity in a world that expects us to constantly give, sacrifice, and endure.

Tricia Hersey, at the Nap Ministry, calls rest a "resistance" to grind culture. For generations, we have lived in survival mode, running on nervous systems wired for high alert. Menopause is a season of transformation — a chance to listen to our bodies, rewrite our narratives, and embrace radical rest as a revolutionary act.

On the back of reading Rest is Resistance: A Manifesto by Tricia Hersey (2022) I created an acronym for myself which I thought that you may find useful:

1. **Prioritise Restful Sleep:**
   Sleep heals. Create bedtime rituals that nurture you — dim the lights, journal, and invite stillness. Your rest is your right.

2. **Build in Daily Relaxation:**
   Menopause invites us to let go of burdens we have carried for too long. As Lorde and Hersey teach, rest is not weakness but a reclamation. Breathe deeply, stretch, or sit in silence to remind yourself you are enough.

3. **Recharge Through Gentle Movement:**
   Move in ways that feel joyful and restorative. Stretch, walk, or sway — let your body guide you to what feels good.

Rest is resistance. Relaxation is radical. Recharge is revolutionary. As we navigate menopause, let us honour ourselves by embracing the rest we have been denied and always deserved.

Leadership Life Lessons for Thriving Through Menopause:

Is My Schedule Enough?

Pouring over my CIPD PM magazine, I came across an interesting double-page article about productivity and how one A-list actor gets through their "punishing" daily schedule. I couldn't help but reflect on how some intense and rigid schedules are portrayed by the media.

As a post-menopausal Black woman and licensed menopause champion, I couldn't help but feel that this article set unrealistic expectations particularly for the menopausal woman juggling work, her health and the demands of a career and CPD studies. I know this only too well from my own upbringing by a single mother who raised three children, worked full-time and studied at night school with no support (I was the oldest, known back then as a 'latchkey kid'). I took care of some domestic duties – no shade on this experience and, through the lens of a young girl, I observed my mother's daily punishing schedule with no support system. While punishing schedules might work for those with few personal responsibilities and a strong support system, for the menopausal woman managing symptoms such as fatigue, brain fog, emotional changes, hot flushes and/or a family, this type of schedule can be harmful. Yet, again, we can often feel the pressure or guilt to meet these standards in fear of somehow feeling that we are not enough.

At the end of this chapter, I have set out for you a personal, tried-and-tested sustainable plan for the menopausal women.

One lesson that resonated deeply was the idea of creating rest boundaries – learning to say "no" without guilt and prioritising what truly matters. Another pivotal point was redefining leadership to include vulnerability, which is something I've often struggled with in environments where I've been a minority. By embracing rest and vulnerability, I've learned to lead not just with strength, but with authenticity and grace.

For Black women, this is a powerful reminder that we don't have to carry the world on our shoulders. For coaches and mentors, it's an invitation to rethink how we guide others by modelling balance and resilience.

Suggested Summary/Actions:

Self-Reflection: Ask yourself, what am I carrying that no longer serves me? Take steps to release unnecessary burdens.

Set Boundaries: Define clear limits that protect your energy and joy. Practice saying no without over explaining.

Prioritise Rest: Schedule downtime as a non-negotiable part of your life. Remember, rest is a form of resistance against burnout.

Share Your Story: Inspire others by sharing your journey of shedding the superwoman cape and stepping into authentic leadership. For example, you could discuss how sharing your own struggles with balancing work and rest has helped others feel seen and encouraged them to set healthy boundaries in their lives.

For readers who may struggle with imposter syndrome and fear being seen or speaking in front of peers, sharing your story can be a powerful enabler. It demonstrates vulnerability and authenticity, showing others that they are not alone in their experiences. To develop presenting skills and overcome this fear, consider starting small: practise in safe environments like supportive groups or with trusted colleagues. Gradually build up to more formal settings. Techniques such as joining a public speaking course, participating in workshops, or seeking mentorship from those who excel in this area can help refine these skills. Remember, presenting is a learned skill that grows with practice and feedback. Embracing this journey can transform a fear into a leadership strength for the future, so consider accessing a coach for this skill set.

Burning Your Superwoman Cape a Five-point Plan for Safe Sustainable Transition

Based on my personal experience throughout my leadership career plan for the menopausal women and highlight the dangers (to my own cost) of maintaining daily punishing regimes during my transitioning through menopause can be an empowering journey, especially when armed with the right tools to combat imposter syndrome and maintain energy levels. Here is a potential five-point plan to keep in mind:

Morning Mindfulness: Start the day with a mindfulness routine. This can include meditation, deep-breathing exercises, or journaling. It helps centre your mind, address feelings of imposter syndrome, and set a positive tone for the day ahead.

Nourishing Nutrition: Focus on a balanced diet rich in essential nutrients. Include plenty of fruits, vegetables, lean proteins, and whole grains. Foods rich in omega-3 fatty acids, such as salmon and flaxseeds, can also help reduce inflammation and improve brain function.

Physical Activity: Engage in regular physical exercise. Whether it is a brisk walk, yoga, or a dance class, staying active not only boosts energy levels but also enhances mood and reduces symptoms of menopause.

Strategic Rest: Incorporate short breaks throughout your day. These micro-breaks can involve stretching, a quick walk, or simply stepping away from your tasks for a few minutes. They can help prevent burnout and maintain consistent energy levels.

Social Support: Build a support network of friends, family, or support groups. Sharing experiences and feelings with others who understand can provide emotional comfort and reduce feelings of isolation.

Remember, it is essential to listen to your body and adapt the plan to suit your unique needs. Every woman's journey through menopause is different, and self-compassion is key. How does this resonate with you?

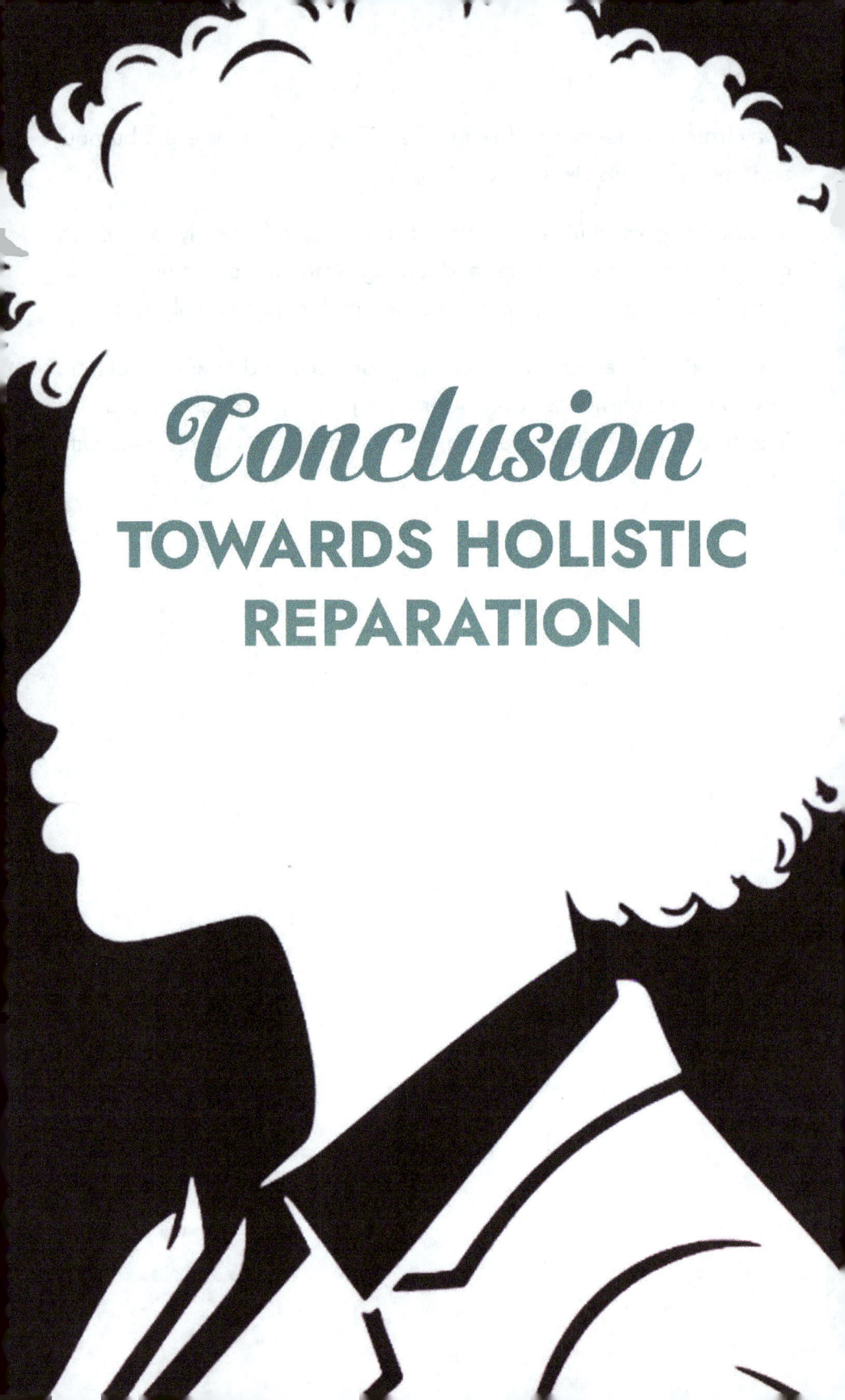

> *"If you don't get out there and define yourself, you'll be quickly and inaccurately defined by others."*
> **Michelle Obama** (Author of Becoming 2018)

As I have moved into my season of holistic reparation, I have been able to deeply reflect through study on my early years and how the subconscious mind can absorb everything around us, shaping how we view ourselves and the world. Dr Bruce Lipton explains in his book *The Biology of Belief* that from birth to about age seven, children operate mostly in a brainwave state like hypnosis, making them highly impressionable. This is when beliefs from family, culture, and society take root. For me, one of those deeply ingrained messages was from my elders, who often said, "You have to work twice as hard to be seen as just as good as your white peers." This was reinforced by the media and the portrayal of Black people, or the lack of their presence as positive role models. While this wisdom and guidance came from a place of love and survival, based on the experiences of my elders on their arrival and treatment in Britain, it also reflected the challenges for me of navigating an unequal socio-economic and societal system. It also created a pressure-filled mindset rooted in perfectionism and the constant need to prove my worth just to feel accepted, valued and heard.

As I grew older, I began to see how limiting this belief system was, and I decided to reprogram my thinking. I study books by thought leaders such as Dr Lipton and Gregg Braden, whose book *The Divine Matrix* helped me understand the power of shifting deeply held beliefs. Through self-reflection, journaling, and affirmations, I gradually replaced the old narrative with a narrative focused on my inherent value — not tied to how hard I worked, how I dressed, how I styled my hair or which postcode I lived in, nor my Lancashire accent. Embracing therapy and setting boundaries for rest and joy were essential steps to deprogram years of being programmed to self-hate. Over time, I realised that breaking free from the need to constantly try to overperform was not just about my own well-being; it was about rejecting systems that thrive on the grind culture and inequalities meted out by those with power and privilege, the white C-suite people. A statement which resonated for me was in the memoir by Michelle Obama, which I have inserted at the beginning of this chapter.

This journey was not easy, but it was transformative. Dr Lipton's and Gregg Braden's teachings provided me with the necessary tools to challenge the old programming and navigate life on my own terms, with less societal pressure and more freedom, leading to finally embracing my creativity that was always there but remained hidden under my Superwoman cape.

Leading with Confidence and Authenticity: Leadership Life Lessons

1. **Reclaim Your Narrative**
   Challenge limiting beliefs and societal expectations. Your worth is not tied to how hard you work or how much you achieve. Focus on owning your story and embracing your unique strengths.

2. **Prioritise Rest and Joy**
   Break free from the Superwoman mindset. Rest is a revolutionary act, especially in systems that expect overwork. Set boundaries and create space for joy — it is essential for sustained leadership.

3. **Cultivate a Support Network**
   Surround yourself with a tribe of mentors, peers, and allies

who understand your journey. Lean on them for advice, encouragement, and collaboration. You do not have to lead alone.

4. **Know When to Say No**
   Not every opportunity is the right one. Saying no to what does not align with your goals or values is a powerful way to preserve energy and focus on what matters most.

5. **Invest in Your Growth**
   Take time to develop your skills and knowledge. Whether it is reading, attending workshops, or seeking mentorship, investing in yourself is a commitment to your long-term success.

6. **Challenge Systems, Not Just Yourself**
   Leadership is not just about personal success — it is about creating change. Use your voice to advocate for equity and fairness within the structures you operate in.

7. **Lead with Authenticity**
   Embrace the fullness of your identity. Whether it is your natural hair, cultural expressions, or lived experiences, bring your authentic self to the table. It is your superpower.

8. **Celebrate Small Wins**
   Leadership is a journey, not a race. Acknowledge your progress, no matter how small. Every step forward is a victory.

9. **Practice Radical Self-Compassion**
   Be as kind to yourself as you are to others. Leadership can be challenging, but you do not have to have all the answers all the time. Give yourself grace.

10. **Redefine Success on Your Terms**
    Do not let traditional definitions of success dictate your path. Define what success looks like for you — whether it is impact, balance, or freedom — and pursue it unapologetically.

Reparations for Black women should address these intersecting layers of oppression by investing in holistic healthcare, including mental health resources, support for menopausal women, and culturally competent care that acknowledges the unique challenges they face. It also involves dismantling harmful stereotypes like the Superwoman trope, which imposes unrealistic expectations and denies Black women the right to be vulnerable, to rest, and to prioritise their own well-being.

By addressing the compounded effects of racism, sexism, health disparities, and the pressure to conform to destructive cultural tropes, reparations can move beyond compensation to include genuine healing, empowerment, and systemic transformation.

> **R.E.S.T. Acronym:**
>
> **R**ecognise your limits: Say no without guilt. Your energy is sacred.
>
> **E**stablish boundaries: rest is not earned; it is necessary.
>
> **S**chedule downtime: make rest a ritual, not an afterthought.
>
> **T**ake small steps: radical rest starts with one pause at a time.

Definitions

In writing this book, I recognised the importance of providing clarity around certain key terms and concepts that are central to the discussions within these pages. Terms like *intersectionality*, *reparation*, and *systemic racism* hold deep, nuanced meanings essential to understanding the lived experiences of Black women, particularly in the context of imposter syndrome. To ensure that all readers – regardless of their familiarity with these concepts – can engage fully with the material, I have created a dedicated section that defines and contextualises these terms as they are used throughout the book. This section serves as a reference point, designed to offer deeper insight and support a shared understanding of the language that shapes the narrative and themes explored.

Affective Labour

Refers to work that involves managing and producing emotional or interpersonal experiences. This type of labour focuses on feelings, relationships, and the emotional well-being of others, often blending with physical or cognitive work. It can include activities like providing care, fostering positive customer interactions, or creating a welcoming environment. Affective labour is especially prominent in sectors like healthcare, education, service industries, and social media. The term highlights how emotional effort is commodified in capitalist systems, where emotions become a resource to enhance productivity or customer satisfaction. For instance, nurses offering compassionate care or retail employees maintaining a cheerful demeanour are examples of affective labour.

Critiques of affective labour often emphasise how it is undervalued, disproportionately performed by women, and frequently overlooked in traditional measures of economic output.

Allyship

- **Women of colour** – defined as a group of women belonging to a racial and ethnic minority group often in the context of society but not limited to Black, Asian, Middle

Eastern dual heritage, Italian. The term acknowledges a shared experience of systematic inequality, discrimination, and marginalisation.

- **"Code-Switching"** reference has been made to the term — alternating between two or more dialects, or cultural behaviours depending on the social context or environment. For many women of colour particularly within academic and professional settings, this can involve how we speak, dress or behave to conform to the exceptions of the dominant culture.

- **Institutional Racism:** Systemic inequities create an environment where Black women must navigate constant obstacles and biases, impacting their mental health, economic opportunities, and overall well-being. Understanding and addressing institutional racism from the perspective of Black women is crucial in fostering genuine equality and justice in society. Institutional racism refers to the policies, practices, and cultural norms embedded within organisations and systems that disproportionately disadvantage Black women and other marginalised groups. Unlike overt acts of individual racism, institutional racism is often subtle, systemic, and deeply ingrained in structures of power. This form of racism is perpetuated through a lack of representation, biased recruitment and promotion practices, inadequate support systems, and an overall disregard for the unique challenges faced by Black women in the workplace.

- **Intersectionality:** The theory of intersectionality, coined by Professor Kimberlé Crenshaw, highlights how various forms of discrimination (such as racism, sexism, ageism, and classism) overlap and compound each other, creating unique challenges for those who sit at the intersection of multiple marginalised identities. For Black women, these intersecting oppressions are not merely additive but create a distinct and compounded experience of marginalisation. Black women navigate a world where their race, gender, and other identities simultaneously impact their social, economic, and health outcomes. A framework for understanding how different aspects of a person's social and political identities intersect to create unique experiences of discrimination and privilege.

- **Mammy-fication:** A harmful social construct that perpetuates the exploitation of Black women by limiting their identities to self-sacrificing caregivers.

- **Microaggression:** Through the lens of the Black woman's experience, microaggressions are subtle, often unintentional forms of discrimination or prejudice that manifest in everyday interactions. These behaviours or comments may seem innocuous or even complimentary to those delivering them, but they carry underlying assumptions and biases that reflect systemic stereotypes, often targeting aspects of a Black woman's identity, such as her race, gender, or both.

Examples of Microaggressions Specific to Black women:
1. **Assumptions About Competence**: A Black woman in a professional setting may be mistaken for a junior staff member, even when she holds a senior position. Comments like, Oh, you're the manager? I did not expect that! reflect a biased perception of what leadership should look like.

2. **Hair Policing**: Comments on natural hairstyles like braids, 'fros, or locs, such as Is that your real hair? or Your hair is so interesting, can I touch it? These remarks, while often framed as curiosity, can feel invasive and reduce Black women's hair to an exotic spectacle rather than an expression of identity.

3. **The Angry Black Woman Trope**: When a Black woman is assertive or expresses strong emotions, she is often labelled as angry or aggressive while the same behaviour might be seen as confident in others. Statements like, "Calm down", "No need to get so angry."

- **Pardner/Sou-Sou:** the Caribbean banking concept of 'Pardner money' (also known as 'Partner', 'Sus', or 'Sou-sou') is an informal, community-based savings system that Caribbean immigrants brought with them when they moved to Britain in the 1950s and 1960s. This practice was rooted in African traditions and became a critical financial tool for many Caribbean communities facing economic challenges in the UK.

- **Reparation:** Refers to actions or measures taken to address and redress historical or ongoing injustices, harms, or damages inflicted upon individuals or communities. Often associated with the legacies of slavery, colonialism, or systemic discrimination, reparations aim to acknowledge wrongdoing, provide compensation, and restore dignity to those who have been wronged. Reparations can take various forms, including financial compensation, public apologies, policy reforms, educational initiatives, land restitution, or programmes designed to promote equity and opportunity. The concept is rooted in justice and accountability, emphasising the need to repair relationships, rectify systemic harm, and create conditions for healing and reconciliation.

- **Superwoman Schema**: A concept popularised by Dr Cheryl L. Woods-Giscombe, a professor at the University of North Carolina, Chapel Hill School of Nursing who introduced the Superwoman Schema (SWS), which highlights the expectations placed on Black women to exude strength, succeed despite limitations, and help others at the expense of their own well-being.

- **The Strong Black Woman Schema (SBW)** is a cultural phenomenon where Black women are expected to be strong, resilient and self-sacrificing, often at the expense of their own mental, emotional, and physical well-being. This stereotype glorifies the image of Black women as inherently capable of managing all forms of adversity, without showing vulnerability or seeking support.

- **Systemic Racism:** Also known as institutional racism, it refers to the deeply embedded policies, practices, and cultural norms within institutions and societies that result in unequal access to resources, opportunities, and rights based on race. Unlike individual acts of prejudice, systemic racism operates through structures of power – such as education, healthcare, criminal justice, housing, and employment – that perpetuate racial disparities and maintain the privilege of dominant racial groups. This form of racism is often subtle and normalised, making it harder to identify and address. It is sustained by historical legacies of colonialism, slavery, and segregation, as well as contemporary policies and practices that disproportionately disadvantage marginalised racial groups, regardless of individual intentions or awareness. Recognising systemic racism is essential for creating equitable systems and dismantling racial inequities.

- **Theory of Change:** A theoretical framework used to provide a comprehensive explanation and illustration of how and why a desired change is expected to happen in a particular context. A Theory of Change outlines steps needed to achieve long-term goals and identifies the relationships between activities, outputs, and outcomes.

Trope: A commonly recurring theme, motif, or literary device used in storytelling, art, or media. It can refer to a specific type of character, which is widely recognised and understood by audiences due to its frequent use.

For example:

- In discussions, "trope" can also highlight patterns or clichés that reflect cultural stereotypes.

- Tropes can be neutral, creative tools, but they may also reinforce negative stereotypes.

- **"Unconscious Bias":** Reference has been made to the term — the automatic and unintentional bias stereotypes or attitudes that affect our understanding and actions and decisions formed through societal influences, and cultural conditioning operating without us being consciously aware.

- **White Saviour:** refers to a trope or behaviour pattern where a white individual assumes a self-imposed role of rescuing or aiding people of colour, often in a way that reinforces power imbalances, perpetuates stereotypes, and centres their own perspective or heroism. This dynamic can manifest in various contexts, such as charity, development work, activism, or storytelling, where the efforts of the 'saviour' overshadow the agency, voices, and lived experiences of those they claim to help. The term critiques the paternalistic and often self-serving motivations behind such actions, highlighting how they can inadvertently sustain systemic inequalities instead of addressing the root causes of oppression. It calls for a shift from saviourism to allyship, which prioritises partnership, humility, and empowering marginalised communities on their own terms.

- **White Fragility:** A term coined by sociologist Robin DiAngelo to describe the discomfort, defensiveness, or emotional reaction that many white individuals exhibit when confronted with discussions about racism, privilege, or their role in systemic inequities. This reaction can manifest as anger, denial, guilt, silence, or withdrawal, and often serves to derail or shut down constructive conversations about race. White fragility stems from living in environments where racial comfort is the norm, leaving individuals ill-equipped to engage in challenging or honest dialogue about racial issues. It perpetuates racial inequality by prioritising the emotional comfort of white individuals over the lived realities and needs of people of colour, thereby maintaining the status quo of systemic oppression.

- **Woke**: Originally emerged from African American vernacular and it referred to being 'awake' or conscious of social and political injustices, particularly those related to systemic racism and inequality. Historically, it encouraged individuals to remain aware of and engaged with social justice issues.

Over time, the term gained mainstream usage and came to broadly signify awareness of a range of social justice causes, including racial equality, gender equity, LGBTQ+ rights, and environmental issues. Being 'woke' implied a commitment to challenging oppression and advocating for equity and inclusion.

However, in recent years, the term has also been co-opted and polarised in public discourse. Some use woke critically or pejoratively to label individuals or movements they perceive as excessively focused on political correctness or ideological activism. This shift has sparked debates about its meaning and the societal pushback against social justice movements.

Despite these changes, its original intent remains a call to stay informed and engaged in combating societal inequities and systemic challenges for Black and brown women working within many systems. One example is the policing of Black hair in corporate spaces. Rooted in white-Eurocentric standards, over the years professional environments have often deemed straightened or Eurocentric hairstyles as more acceptable while stigmatising natural Black hair textures, braids, locs, and other styles intrinsic to Black identity and this has unwittingly been done through workforce policies namely uniform and workwear policies. The British Dove research on Black hair underscores this disparity, revealing that Black women are significantly more likely to experience microaggressions, discrimination, and exclusion from the workplace due to their hair.

Despite many organisations publicly championing values of inclusion, belonging, and equity – claiming that "every voice counts" – the lived realities of Black women often contradict these statements. National staff surveys in the UK consistently highlight unequal experiences for staff of colour, including fewer opportunities for advancement and a higher prevalence of bullying and harassment. These disparities reveal the gap between stated values and workplace practices.

The inconsistency is stark: while promoting inclusivity on the surface, these same organisations may enforce policies or foster cultures that marginalise Black women, particularly regarding their hair and broader expressions of identity. Gaslighting frequently compounds this issue, with Black women's challenges dismissed as minor grievances, further entrenching feelings of invisibility and alienation.

For Black women in corporate spaces, these experiences exacerbate the psychological toll of navigating a system that demands overperformance and conformity to whiteness. They often feel the need to dilute their identity to be deemed 'professional' while simultaneously hearing rhetoric about diversity and belonging that does not translate into equitable outcomes. True inclusion requires dismantling these biases, valuing the authenticity of Black women – including their hair – and creating environments where belonging is a reality, not just a slogan.

Tackling White Supremacy

Strategic Recommendations for Organisations

Revise Policies and Standards:
Eliminate language and practices in dress codes or grooming policies that discriminate against Black hair and cultural expression.

Adopt inclusive policies that affirm the acceptability of all hairstyles, including 'fros, braids, locs, and twists.

Education and Training:
Implement mandatory anti-racism and cultural competency training for all staff, focusing on unconscious bias, microaggressions, cultural identity, and health disparities working with members of local community or patient by experience.

Educate leaders and managers specifically on the significance of Black hair and headdress with specific relevance to religious identity and belonging.

Data Transparency:
Analyse workforce data from staff surveys and exit interviews to identify disparities in experiences and opportunities for employees of colour.

Publish metrics on equity, and inclusion EDI initiatives and track progress toward equitable representation at all levels.

Accountability Structures:
Establish clear mechanisms for reporting and addressing discrimination and bullying, ensuring complaints are taken seriously and resolved effectively.

Appoint senior EDI leaders with the authority to enforce change and align organisational practices with inclusion goals.

Representation and Mentorship:
Prioritise hiring and promoting Black employees into leadership roles to reflect diversity at decision-making levels.

Create mentorship programs that support career advancement for Black staff, with a focus on navigating and thriving in professional environments.

Create Safe Spaces:
Support employee staff resource groups for Black employees, allowing them to share experiences, advocate for change, and foster community.

Provide forums for open dialogue where Black staff can express concerns without fear of retribution.

Embed Inclusion into Core Values:
Go beyond lanyards and slogans and align EDI efforts with organisational values and strategic objectives.

Highlight and celebrate cultural diversity in workplace events and communications.

About the Author

Beverley is a Licensed Menopause Champion, Accredited Life Coach, and strategic leader with over two decades of experience spanning public and private sectors. She holds an MSc in Diversity Strategic Management, a Postgraduate Certificate in Education, and a degree in Social Policy, Welfare, and Diversity—credentials that underpin her evidence-based, practical approach to leadership, inclusion, and wellbeing.

Before establishing her reputation in public service, Beverley spent several years in the commercial sector, excelling in sales and management at one of the UK's top high street fashion stores. This experience gave her first-hand insight into workplace dynamics, customer engagement, and leadership under pressure, which she now translates into coaching and organisational guidance.

As founder of *Rest Rise Reclaim*, Beverley empowers women to shed societal expectations, embrace their authentic selves, and lead on their own terms. Her debut book, *Rest, Rise, Reclaim: Leadership Life Lessons for women of colour* draws on her personal and professional journey to help women navigate menopause, overcome self-doubt, and achieve fulfilment and leadership renewal this book is also for the young Black girl who maybe seeking a career and not yet made a clear decision.

Through coaching, workshops, and speaking engagements, Beverley inspires women to reclaim their power, embrace identity, and make meaningful impact. Her work is grounded in resilience, authenticity, and empathy—providing practical strategies to thrive in both career and life.

Additional Resources

House of Commons Library. *Prison Statistics, England and Wales.* Research Briefing, 6 December 2017.

Ministry of Justice. *Prison Population Projections 2009–2015, England and Wales.* Statistics Bulletin, 28 August 2009.

Keith, Sir Brian. *Report of the Zahid Mubarek Inquiry.* Vols. 1 and 2, HC 1082, The Stationery Office, 29 June 2006. Available at: https://www.gov.uk/government/publications/report-of-the-zahid-mubarek-inquiry

The Secret Policeman: Racism Uncovered at National Police Training School. BBC, October 2003.

Police Face Action After BBC Racism Film. The Guardian, 4 March 2005. https://www.theguardian.com/

Dear Reader,

As you reach the end of *Rest Rise Reclaim*, I want to acknowledge the rich tapestry of wisdom and experience that has shaped this work. The **additional resources** offer further insights and context to broaden your understanding of the important themes we have explored together, and the following **bibliography** highlights the key books, reports, and voices that have deeply influenced my journey and thinking.

I invite you to use these references not only as tools for knowledge but as sources of encouragement and empowerment on your own leadership path. May they inspire you to rise, reclaim, and lead with courage and clarity.

Thank you for joining me on this journey.

Research the Organisation:

Look at public commitments to EDI, representation at leadership levels, and responses to diversity-related controversies.

Review policies on grooming and cultural expression to assess alignment with your identity.

Speak to Employees:
Reach out to current or former Black employees to understand their experiences. Employee resource groups can be a good entry point.

Check EDI Metrics and Initiatives:
Investigate whether the organisation publishes data on diversity or reports on its EDI goals and achievements.

Observe Leadership Representation:
Evaluate if Black professionals are represented in senior positions or visible roles within the organisation.

Know Your Worth:
Be clear on your career goals, non-negotiables, and personal values to assess if the organisation's culture and opportunities align with your aspirations.

Ask Direct Questions in Interviews:
Inquire about the company's approach to EDI, mentoring, and managing bias or discrimination in the workplace.

Trust Your Instincts:
If interactions during the hiring process feel dismissive, patronising, or insincere about inclusivity, consider it a red flag.

Build Your Network:
Seek out external support networks of Black professionals to share experiences and advice.

Initiative-taking steps; organisations can create equitable environments, and Black employees can navigate their careers with clarity and confidence.

Bibliography

The following selected books, articles, reports, and media sources have informed and inspired the themes explored in this book. They are included here for readers who wish to deepen their understanding.

Books

Abbott, Diane. A Woman Like Me. Penguin Books, 2019.

Angelou, Maya. I Know Why the Caged Bird Sings. Random House, 1969.

Braden, Gregg. The Divine Matrix: Bridging Time, Space, Miracles, and Belief. Hay House,

2007.

Carey Yazeed, C. Stop Telling Black Women to Be Strong! Yana Publishing, 2019.

DiAngelo, Robin. White Fragility: Why It's So Hard for White People to Talk About Racism.

Beacon Press, 2018.

Elle, Alexandra. How We Heal: Uncover Your Power and Set Yourself Free. Chronicle Books,

2022.

Hersey, Tricia. Rest Is Resistance: A Manifesto. Melville House, 2022.

hooks, bell. Sisters of the Yam: Black Women and Self-Recovery. South End Press, 1993.

hooks, bell. Talking Back: Thinking Feminist, Thinking Black. South End Press, 1989.

Lipton, Bruce H. The Biology of Belief: Unleashing the Power of Consciousness, Matter, and

Miracles. Hay House, 2005.

Lorde, Audre. Sister Outsider: Essays and Speeches. Crossing Press, 1984.

Maté, Gabor. When the Body Says No: Exploring the Stress—Disease Connection. Vintage

Canada, 2003.

Morrison, Toni. Song of Solomon. Alfred A. Knopf, 1977.

Obama, Michelle. Becoming. Crown Publishing Group, 2018.

Scott, Keisha. Black Women's Strategy: Love. (Publication details forthcoming).

Journal Articles

Avis, N. E., Crawford, S. L., Greendale, G., Bromberger, J. T., Everson-Rose, S. A., Gold, E.

B., Hess, R., Joffe, H., Kravitz, H. M., & Tepper, P. G. "Differences in Menopausal

Symptoms Across Ethnic Groups." Menopause, 22(6), 2015, pp. 623–630.

Berk, Lee S., and Stanley A. Tan. "The Neuroscience and Humour-Induced Modulation of

Immunity." Alternative Therapies in Health and Medicine, 1988.

Crenshaw, Kimberlé. "Demarginalizing the Intersection of Race and Sex: A Black Feminist

Critique of Antidiscrimination Doctrine, Feminist Theory and Antiracist Politics." University

of Chicago Legal Forum, Vol. 1989, Issue 1, pp. 139–167.

Crenshaw, Kimberlé. "Mapping the Margins: Intersectionality, Identity Politics, and Violence

against Women of Color." Stanford Law Review, 43(6), 1991, pp. 1241–1299.

Woods-Giscombé, Cheryl L. "Superwoman Schema: African American Women's Views on

Stress, Strength, and Health." Qualitative Health Research, 20(5), 2010.

Reports & Inquiries

Adichie, Chimamanda Ngozi. "The Danger of a Single Story." TED Talk, 2009.

British Heart Foundation. Cardiovascular Disease in Black Women. British Heart

Foundation, 2021.

Fawcett Society. Menopause and the Workplace: The Impact on Women of Colour. Fawcett

Society, 2022.

House of Commons Library. Prison Statistics, England and Wales. Research Briefing, 6

December 2017.

Keith, Sir Brian. Report of the Zahid Mubarek Inquiry. Vols. 1 and 2, HC 1082. London: The

Stationery Office, 29 June 2006. Available at:

https://www.gov.uk/government/publications/report-of-the-zahid-mubarek-inquiry

Macpherson, William. The Stephen Lawrence Inquiry: Report of an Inquiry by Sir William

Macpherson of Cluny. London: The Stationery Office, 1999.

Ministry of Justice. Prison Population Projections 2009–2015, England and Wales. Statistics

Bulletin, 28 August 2009.

SWAN (Study of Women's Health Across the Nation). SWAN Report. Pittsburgh: University of Pittsburgh, 1995.

United Kingdom. The Zahid Mubarek Inquiry: Report of the Zahid Mubarek Inquiry. London: The Stationery Office, 2006.

Media Sources

The Secret Policeman: Racism Uncovered at National Police Training School. BBC, October 2003.

Police Face Action After BBC Racism Film. The Guardian, 4 March 2005. Available at:

https://www.theguardian.com/heading

www.marciampublishing.com

www.ingramcontent.com/pod-product-compliance
Lightning Source LLC
Chambersburg PA
CBHW052020070526
44584CB00016B/1830